# ADULT PARTICIPATION
# IN SWEDISH HIGHER EDUCATION

## A Study of Organizational Structure, Educational Design and Current Policies

### kenneth
### Abrahamsson

ALMQVIST & WIKSELL INTERNATIONAL STOCKHOLM

This book reports a case study on adult participation in Swedish higher education. The study has been done within the CERI project on Innovations in Higher Education and formed part of a comparative study on Financial and Organizational Policies and Practices regarding Adults in Higher Education (the other countries were Austria, Canada, France, Federal Republic of Germany, UK, USA and Japan). Some of these studies has been reported by Hans G. Schütze (ed.) *Adults in Higher Education. Policies and Practice in the United Kingdom and North America.* Almqvist & Wiksell International (forthcoming volume).

Further copies of these two books may be requested through Almqvist & Wiksell International, P. O. Box 638, S-101 28 Stockholm, Sweden.

© Kenneth Abrahamsson and NBUC
Produced for Almqvist & Wiksell International by
PAN EIDOS, Lund, Sweden.
Typesetting by MICROMAX, Lund.
Printed by Novapress, Lund.
Almqvist & Wiksell International, Stockholm, Sweden, 1986
ISBN 91-22-00850-0
ISSN 0280-2988

# Contents

# Foreword

The purpose of this study is to describe the increasing participation of adults in Swedish higher education during the seventies; a process that could be labelled the 'adultification' of higher education. Some of the main questions raised in the report are:

• Which are the general determinants of this so called adultification of higher education?
• Which are the main policy ideas and organizational instruments relating to adult participation and recurrent education? How do we assess the impact of this policy?
• What kind of conflicts and tensions are raised by the 'adult majority' in Swedish higher education; e.g. balance between young students and adults, academic ideals and vocational up-grading, short cycle courses and degree programmes etc
• And finally, what have we learnt about adults in higher education and the idea of recurrent education, ten years after the political decision of reforming Swedish higher education

It is not easy to present simple answers to these complex questions or issues. When I started writing in the end of 1982, I was stimulated by the notion of adultification. Two or three years later it seems more suitable to use the methaphor 'the declining adult majority' in Swedish higher education. Once again we are facing shifting political ideals and a new reality. Youth unemployment and the interest in future options of young students, especially in the context of a newly started reform work in the field of upper secondary education, have a higher priority than adult education in general, at the level of higher education in particular.

Looking back in the Swedish policy mirror, it is easy to see that the seventies comprised a reform-intensive decade. Apart from the new developments in higher education, a number of adult education reforms passed the Swedish parliament (Riksdagen); i.e. a law of educational leave of absence, a new system of grants and loans to finance studies, priority measures for underprivileged groups. Unfortunately, the implementation of the reforms started in a period of economic stagnation and fiscal crises. Another factor that is important to mention in an international context, is the change of governments between 1976 and 1982. The reform ideas were developed in a progressive and expanding educational climate, while the implementation took place in a more restrictive political and financial climate. Thus, it is not easy to discuss the conditions of reform evaluation, when the contexts of implementation are shifting.

This effort to present organizational and financial policies and some of the main trends in participation in Swedish adult higher education is not a result of primary research and new data collection. Rather, my ambition has mainly been to put together empirical data that is already available in national statistics, special investigations and, of course, reports from projects which have been part of the Swedish programme to follow-up the reform of higher education in 1977.

The theme of adult students in higher education is a fascinating one, which reflects subjects such as mid-career change, dreams and disappointments, experiential sharing in an academic context, study skills and study patterns, drop-in, drop-out and why not drop-by. I wish that I would have had more time to spend on these issues. The time budget of a civil servant is, however, restricted and somewhat controlled. In this situation of cross pressure, which I share with most adult students, I am grateful for being able to rely on the knowledge and professional competence of persons such as Marianne Bauer, Agneta Bladh, Urban Dahllöf, Lillemor Kim, Lennart Levin, Inger Marklund, Kjell Rubenson, Allan Svensson, Magnus Söderström, Erik Tängdén, Staffan Wahlén and Hans-Erik Östlund. I also wish to thank Hans G. Schütze, CERI/OECD for his interest in the Swedish case and in the development of this report and Susan Opper for valuable comments on the final draft.

Stockholm in December 1985
*Kenneth Abrahamsson*

2

# 1      An introductory comment

## Policy concepts in a comparative context

Any attempt to clarify and compare the level and pattern of adult participation in higher education in different countries has to start with a general discussion of objectives, terms and useful categories. The country survey document provided by the secretariat offers a general and practical outline, which, however, has to be interpreted and adjusted to different national settings and more or less country-specific conditions (see Appendix 4). It is not difficult to find arguments for including Sweden in the current CERI-study on organizational and financial policies relating to the participation of adults in higher education in France, the USA, U.K., and Federal Republic of Germany.

Sweden is a country with a long tradition in adult education, although the more organized effort in the field of adult higher education is a post-war product (if one excludes the university extention movement which has its roots back in the late 19th century). Sweden is also interesting as a change agent in the 'Open Door Policy' that became so common in some western countries during the seventies. Further, the reform of higher education of 1977, where the notion of recurrent education and the aim of better links to working life were integral parts, are other reasons for taking the Swedish case as one of the examples in this study.

A comparison of the participation level in adult higher education in various countries cannot only be made from the formal characteristics of the different educational systems. One also has to take into consideration how programme design and study patterns work in practice. It is not too challenging a hypothesis to assume that the differences in educational design and student behaviour between various western countries will be smaller if we look to what is really happening and not only to the formal policy images of the systems of higher education.

A major distinction is made between adults participating in degree oriented programmes on the one hand and adult students in continuing higher education on the other hand. On a general level, this distinction seems to be applicable in different national settings. Looking closer at the problem, however, it is not always easy to judge what is a good degree oriented programme for adult students and what constitutes further education. It is not only a question of choosing between a prefabricated core curriculum and an individually determined 'cafeteria-approach' (defined by a set of separate courses). Rather we have to find different solutions relating to various groups of adult students. Thus we must incorporate a whole range of students from "second chance" students with a restricted educational background to students with substantial professional and educational experiences. It is also necessary to find new ways of categorizing higher education curricula so it reflects the needs not only of adults, but the expectations of more heterogeneous student populations. Further, new relationships and new contracts between higher education and working life call for special attention to non-formal adult higher education and to adult education in general.

If we take the Swedish integrated system of higher education as an example, the distinction between general study programmes and separate or single courses is an equivalent to the degree programme-continuing education dichotomy on the theoretical level. In practice, however, adult students with substantial professional experience might benefit from an individually designed curriculum thereby trying to mix professional competence and higher learning. The North American experiments of recognizing prior learning (so called RPL-programmes) provide one model of discussing this problem.[1] The idea of a core curriculum, applied in general degree-oriented programmes tends to favour the institutions's academic ideals instead of the students' needs. Thus, we cannot simply take the ideas, terms and categories developed for traditional students and apply them to a discussion of the conditions of adult higher education. In addition, it has to be said that the distinction between 'credit' and 'non-credit' higher education has different meanings in different countries. A formal distinction in the Swedish system of higher education is made between general (mainly degree oriented) programmes and so called separate or single courses. In reality, however, the concept is not so clear, and general study programmes and separate courses sometimes overlap as a student taking separate courses can take a complete degree by combining different subject courses. Further, it is necessary to look more closely at local study programmes and individualized programmes of higher learning in Sweden.

Another crucial distinction could be drawn between policies and practices. From a theoretical point of view, few countries tend to have more organized and coherent national policies to meet the needs and demands of adults in higher education. The lack of a codified national policy to meet the adult needs does not necessarily lead to bad or underdeveloped practices in this field. The vast numbers of entrepreneurial experiments and organizational ideas in the field of higher learning in the US are evidence enough. And beyond all policies and structures there are various patterns of individuals with different motives, study projects and life conditions.

On the other hand, in countries with more codified policies of adult participation in higher education, such as Sweden and the UK, these policies can provide quite different solutions both in relation to level of participation and organizational structures. Typical for the integrated system of higher education in Sweden is that we work with heterogeneous student groups and that there are no specific curricula or classes which are open only to adult students. Our 'Open Door policy', does not include an Open University model with a nation-wide system of distance education, but a specific access channel for adult students with work experience in the admission to all programmes and courses. Thus, the level of adult participation must be analyzed in the context of different organizational and structural solutions as well as different methods of resource allocation.

Thirdly, the level and pattern of adult participation in higher education has to be related to objectives and educational ideals of higher learning. One of the experiences of the Klagenfurt-seminar, organized by CERI/OECD, 'Adult students – a challenge to universities' was that the policy discussion in 'low level participation'-countries showed marked differences with the policy-debate in 'high level participation'-countries.[2] In Sweden, which is an example of the latter, it is evident that the main policy interest today is not a further opening up of the system for adult students, but to give the young students better chances in the admission process. Two of the most obvious signs of this new policy are the parliamentary decision to change the relative weight of work experience in the admission (from 2.5 point of 7.5 possible to 1.7 of 6.7 possible) and the broadening of the access channels for young students from upper secondary school level (from 20% to 33%).[3] Admission and selection are important policy issues in Swedish higher education. The organization of the Swedish admission system has also become the task of a government commission.[4]

Taking the increased competition between young and adult students into account, it is not surprising to note that a final report of the Swedish admission project did not deal with problems of adult students, but with the conditions of 'direct students' and their transition from upper secondary school to higher education.[5] This competition for places has also to be considered in the context of both youth unemployment and economic stagnation and a more restrictive public budget.

The shift in priorities from adult students to young students has also to be viewed in relation to the changed political situation in Sweden in the mid-seventies. When the parliament voted for the reform in 1975 Sweden had a social democratic government. As a consequence of the general election of 1976, the social democrats lost their majority and three new governments were set up by the center party (former farmers' party), the liberals and the conservative party during 1976 and 1982. In retrospect, one could say that the new parliament situation increased the political orientation towards higher education for young people. Thus, the reform strategy was created during one regime, while the implementation in 1977 took part in a new political context with a new regime. In general, it is also possible to say that the cut backs between 1979 and 1982 had stronger effects on adult education than on education for young people. On the other hand it is obvious that Sweden, in a comparative perspective, had reached a broad provision of adult education in the late seventies.

## The 'adultification' of Swedish higher education

The so called 'adultification' of the Swedish system of higher education, where students above 25 years of age are in the majority in many degree programmes and most separate courses, does not mainly imply strong participation of so called underprivileged adults with a restricted educational background.[6] Rather, a number of adults tend to be educationally well-equipped as far as both qualified professional experiences and prior schooling are concerned. This is very significant as far as degree-programmes are concerned (where only 5% of newly enrolled students embark on the so called 25:4 scheme, which forms a main part of the Swedish Open Door Policy; see Appendix 1: "The organization of Swedish higher education). It is less true of separate courses, where almost half of the students are admitted according to the work experience route. Although the 25:4-scheme is still an important policy issue, there is an increasing policy interest in the more qualified adult student. Thus, the government bill of

6

education for fiscal year 1983/84 stresses the need of professional up-grading.[7]

Further, a comparison of the level and pattern of adult participation in higher education in different countries can not only be made with consideration to *external determinants* such as the labour market, the economy, educational leave, study finance, guidance and social support, provision of other forms of adult education and access channels e.g. the broadening of upper secondary schooling.

Attention has also to be paid to *internal determinants* i.e. instrumental and environmental aspects of the organization of schools of higher education. By instrumental we mean mechanisms that select, control and support the individual adult student's progress and failure in the system. Traditional measures in this field are ways of adopting and accepting new students, teaching methods, retention strategies such as counselling and educational support during the study, ethos and institutional value-structure, patterns of participation in programme design and evaluation. The more we open up our systems of higher education, the greater the need for knowing about and controlling these internal determinants.

There are marked differences in patterns of adopting and accepting new adult students in different western countries. In Sweden the potential student does not primarily apply to a university or a college, but to one or more study programmes or single courses. Once a student has been admitted to a programme there is usually no assessment of his subject knowledge or study skill. On a voluntary basis, adult applicants can take a general aptitude test (högskoleprovet), which is not, however, related to any specific subject.

Adult students above 25 years of age and with at least four years of work experience are eligible for higher studies. In the selection process, however, information is gathered from three sources. Firstly, the adult student can get up to 1.7 points for work experience. Secondly, he or she will recognize up to 2.0 points for the aptitude test. And, thirdly the student has to meet requirements of specific subject knowledge in many general study pro-grammes and some separate courses. The specific entrance requirements close 'the open door' to a large extent. Further, it is evident that most 25:4-scheme students aiming at general study programmes with selected admission have to take the aptitude test. In addition, we must mention that there is a specific admission procedure for separate courses.

Typical for the Swedish way of using both work experience and the aptitude test is that they are mainly used for admission and selection, while functions such as diagnosis and learning seem to be neglected. Thus, it is formal merits (marks in upper secondary school and work experience points or work experience points together with the test score), that will be criteria of success or failure. In many institutions of higher learning in the US, the student is normally admitted to a specific university or a college, and he has to go through a rather intensive procedure of assessment, interviewing, counselling and recognition of prior experiences, before a decision is made as to what programme and level he will embark on. Even if the assessment procedure tends to be more formalized at bigger universities, US higher education is still characterized by a more individualized admission process than the Swedish system. The different ways of controlling and supporting the individual learning process cannot only be analyzed from didactic or psychological frames of reference, they also reflect the organizational structure and values of different systems of higher education.

# 2     Did Sweden have adult students prior to the reform of 1977?

## Adult students – a footnote in Swedish educational history?

Writing nearly 60 years ago, when university and college admissions in Sweden were, in relation to the national population, barely one tenth of the figure today, the popular Swedish educator, Oscar Olsson, declared:

> The advent of democracy has thoroughly transformed social conditions. It is becoming obvious to progressively wider circles that people in all walks of life are not just practitioners in need of vocational training for the sake of their independent livelihood but also citizens in need of general education so as to be able to exercise their rights and discharge their duties in public life in a responsible manner. Is everybody, then, to receive a university education? No, but everybody who feels the need for university education and is prepared to make the necessary sacrifices and perform the necessary labour in order to enjoy it. In return for this contribution to life as a fully paid-up member of society and civilised being, the worker should be just as entitled as the poor. The class-conscious worker of our age is not at all disposed to acknowledge that he and his children are in some way by nature duty-bound to become more ignorant, stupid and base than the children of the wealthy, simply because the wealthy can afford to buy the best educational opportunities for their children's intellectual and moral development and refinement.

Nowadays the poor and their children feel that they are just as entitled as anybody else to opportunities of participating in the best of our cultural heritage and the most beautiful, ennobling and truthful achievements of art, literature and science.[1]

So much for 60 years ago. Going still further back in time, we find that education and university studies have always been reserved for the few. Plato's Academy was unmistakably linked with the aristocracy of the time. Its pupils did not include women and slaves. The early Swedish universities recruited most of their students from the aristocracy, but also from the burgesses of the towns and most land-owning classes. Students were admitted at a far more tender age than is now the practice. For example, there were cases of aristocratic 10-year-olds being enrolled at Uppsala University during the seventeenth century. Between 15 and 20% of the students, however, were the sons of farmers – a very high figure by international standards – and so university studies became an important factor of social mobility.[2] It should be borne in mind, however, that throughout the eighteenth century, the non-noble agrarian class and the landless rural and urban proletariat comprised more than 90% of Sweden's population. The middle class existing at the end of the 18th century amounted to some 4%, the nobility 0.5% and the clergy 0.9%.[3] Clearly, then, present-day discussions concerning 'new categories in higher education' are inapplicable to the social conditions of that period.

In a more contemporary perspective, the student population of universities and colleges remained consistently small from the turn of the century until about 1950. It then doubled during the 1950s and tripled during the 1960s, while the 1970s brought an unexpected, steep rise in the proportion of mature students. This dramatic growth in student numbers, combined with the growing heterogeneity of the student population (with age as only one of several criteria), not only made special demands on the outward conditions of higher education, such as localization, scale and the organization of studies. It also both directly and indirectly influenced the inward life of higher education, its content and cognitive definitions, and can with all certainty be expected to continue to do so.

## New and old students

Much of the discussion of Swedish adult higher education takes the reform of 1977 as a point of departure. It is not difficult to find several reasons for this choice. The reform created a new administrative and organizational umbrella of all postsecondary education in Sweden. One of the main ideas behind the reform was a better and more efficient interaction between higher education and working life. At the institutional level, this policy was implemented by a new network of public representatives in programme design and university planning. At the individual level, the recognition of work experience both for young and adult students became an important tool.[4]

The reform can also be seen in the context of an increasing policy interest in working life issues during the seventies. A new working life legislation in the mid-seventies was followed by certain educational measures, e.g. a law of educational leave of absence, a system for study finance for basic adult studies and experiments with out-reach activities in order to meet the needs of the under-educated adults at their own work place.

The strong working life orientation was also reflected in higher education planning, where the idea of recurrent education, i.e. planned alternation between work, education and leisure, formed an integral part of the goal structure. Three central measures have been taken to support the idea of recurrent education within the field of higher education. Firstly, the widened admission scheme (the 25:5-scheme) has been institutionalized through the new admission system with the 25:4-scheme for adults and work experiences as an additional entrance merit for young students. Secondly, the programme structure was redesigned and the idea of separate courses for continuing education needs was developed. Thirdly, it is necessary to mention the idea of dividing longer professionally oriented study programmes into so called phased exits.[5]

It is not possible, however, to point to a direct and causal impact of this policy on the recruitment of adults to Swedish higher education. The growing enrolment of adult students started long before the reform. As Dahllöf has stressed in his well-known re-analysis of a Swedish study on student background in the late sixties, important changes both in age-composition and study patterns occurred in the early sixties.[6] Thus, the reform work in the seventies can be seen as a successive adaptation to a development with roots back in the late fifties. This is, of course, also true for the development of the new admission system. As far as the adult students were concerned the new system rules were an adjustment to previous praxis.[7] The growing demand for adult higher education was also channelled through extramural higher education, where adult students could participate in subject-related university circles and later on get credits through the university-system.

Further, in the years after the reform the student population comprised both students studying according to the previous educational system (i.e. the reform of the programme structure of the faculties of arts and sciences of

1969) and students entering the new system of higher education. Two years after the reform the new Open Door policy was modified by a parliament decision on a numerus clausus and general planning frames defining the number of students in different programmes and courses.

The experiences of the reform implementation have raised the question of the need for other modifications of the original goal structure. In general, one could say, that the reform ideas were developed in a progressive and expanding educational climate, while the implementation took place in a new political climate (with three liberal-conservative governments between 1976 and 1982) and increasing financial restraints due to economic stagnation. In 1980 the Swedish parliament took a decision on reducing the relative weight of work experience in the admission process and to give 'direct students' better opportunities. Between 1979 and 1982, the reform process was studied by a parliamentary commission. Early in 1983 the new government published a discussion report on a number of policy issues in Swedish higher education, some of these issues concerned new forms of public influence in higher education and some unforeseen difficulties in the new programme structure, e.g. that a major portion of the subjects in the field of the humanities are mainly provided as separate courses. In addition to this, it is necessary to mention the government commission on admission to higher education.[8]

## Reform evaluation as a continuing process

This continuous political adjustment between ideals and realities can also be seen as one form of reform evaluation. In addition to this process of policy articulation and policy modification, the National Board of Universities and Colleges (NBUC) has had its own reform evaluation programme, which started in 1976 and has now reached its final phase. The empirical illustrations of this report were mainly built on studies and reports of projects in this reform evaluation programme combined with various sources of Swedish higher education statistics.[9]

One of the objectives of the NBUC reform evaluation programme has been to provide data, results and knowledge on the impact of the organizational tools developed in order to promote the general goal structure of the reform (i.e. the admission system, the programme structure, forms of central and local governance including the balance between public and academic interests, the budget process and activity evaluation). It is difficult and it may be too early to analyze the impact of the evaluation programme on the policy level. There are several explanations for this fact. Firstly, we have not had the final reports of some projects. Secondly, the evaluation programme has had a broader policy orientation including not only the central level, but also the regional and local level. Thirdly, different research methodologies have been tried in the programme.

Thus, over ten years after the publication of the final report of the U 68 commission, ten years after the adoption of a new Higher Education Act in the Swedish parliament and eight years after the first day of the reform implementation (1 July, 1977) there is no general statement of the reform impact. We have studies of the political process leading up to the reform but no comprehensive and far-reaching investigation on the outcome of the reform as far as recruitment, study strategies, student flows, drop-out rates and examination are concerned.[10] In some respects, we tend to know more about the effects of the reform of the programme structure of the faculties of arts and sciences of 1969 than we know and can anticipate to know about the new reform.[11] There are several explanations for this phenomenon.

Firstly, the period after the implementation of the U 68 marks a new policy pattern with more emphasis on continuous and successive modifications than the creation of new organizational systems. Special attention has been paid to curriculum development and programme design within the new organizational context. Secondly, the reform process and the balance between different kinds of interest structures (such as public interests vs academic, liberal education vs professional specialization or skill upgrading, the encounter between academic and non-academic traditions, excellence vs equality) raised the need for value clarification approaches.[12]

Thus, traditional statistical approaches and register analyses had difficulties in competing with the growing interest in and need for qualitative data. In addition, a new law of data-security and personal integrity made it much more difficult to perform quantitative follow-up studies. Another obstacle to qualified statistical approaches was that government delayed its decision on a new administrative system of documentating study patterns (STUDOC).

The issue of adult participation in Swedish higher education is no exception in this respect. It is, of course, possible to outline some general patterns of recruitment and study patterns of adults. Thus, we know that adult students above 25 years of age are in the majority in many programmes and courses in Swedish higher education. In a comparative perspective, this 'adultification' of Swedish higher education is an interesting phenomenon. If we want to analyze problems at a deeper level we still lack sufficient knowledge of main determinants to make valid comparisons between different kinds of adult and young students.

The studies of adult participation in Swedish higher education have mainly focused on problems such as the recruitment effect of different methods of providing higher education outside universities (such as distance education and new forms of extramural higher education), the development of a new admission system with a specific access channel for adults with work experience and the implementation of the idea of recurrent education. We have not been successful in our attempts to acquire a more integrated knowledge of the reform effects, e.g. the interplay between the programme structure and the admission system.

From a bird's-eye view the year 1977 might be seen as the birth of Swedish adult higher education. This is, of course, an over-simplification. In a postwar perspective, one might see the proposal of the U 68 commission and the subsequent parliament decision as an organizational and functional consequence and further development of previous reform work both in higher education and in compulsory and upper secondary education. With the exception of extramural higher education with roots back to the early British University Extension Movement at the end of the last century, the discussions of adult participation in higher education programmes started in the mid-forties and resulted in two main policy solutions.

Firstly, post-war development is accompanied by successive modifications of the admission rules (which culminated in the experiment with widened admissions in 1969 and the new admission system of 1977). Secondly, the educational gap between the young and adult generation should be bridged by the building of special schools for adults aiming at basic knowledge on compulsory and post-compulsory level. In the late sixties, the new schools for adults were transformed into a new system of municipal adult education with the same general curricula as the comprehensive school system.[13]

# 3   Adult participation rate in Swedish higher education – an overview

## Changes over a long term period

We have mentioned earlier that Sweden witnessed a dramatic rise in the number of first-time enrolments of adults in the early seventies. Parallel to this 'adultification' of the system of higher education, there was a decrease in the percentage of young students. We have also pointed to the fact that the increasing enrolments of adults in Swedish higher education is a process that started long before the early seventies. It might be described as a 'latent process' during the fifties, which was more manifest during the sixties and culminated during the seventies. If we exclude former non-academic programmes (which were included in higher education system in 1977), the age structure (including postgraduate students) is as presented in table 3:1 (page 16).

In general, one could say that a measure of 'new enrolments' is a better age-criterion than 'present students' if we want to point to trends over a longer period. The choice of the latter criterion is mainly due to the availability of statistics, and not in order to give the 'best picture'.

The Swedish system of higer education expanded rather slowly up to the beginning of the fifties, doubled during the fifties and almost exploded during the sixties. Figure 3:1 (page 17) illustrates this dramatic development both for young and adult students.

The development during the sixties and seventies cannot be described as

**Table 3:1**   Age-distribution and total number of present students (including post-graduate students) from 1962-1980 in traditional Swedish higher education. Source   *UHÄ-report 1981:18*, page 103.

|  | | | | *Percentage for year* | | | | | |
| Age | 1962 | 1966 | 1970 | 1973 | 1976 | 1977 | 1978 | 1979 | 1980 |
|---|---|---|---|---|---|---|---|---|---|
| -24 | 60 | 66 | 57 | 45 | 41 | 42 | 39 | 38 | 37 |
| 25-34 | 33 | 28 | 36 | 43 | 42 | 39 | 40 | 39 | 40 |
| 35- | 7 | 6 | 7 | 12 | 17 | 19 | 21 | 23 | 23 |
| Total | 44,400 | 76,400 | 123,200 | 110,700 | 113,800 | 120,200 | 129,500 | 126,800 | 130,300 |

Reading this table we must take important distinctions into consideration. We have previously pointed to the distinction between general study programmes and separate courses. In a comparative perspective it is necessary to stress that the general study programmes comprise both traditional higher education (e.g. faculties of arts and science, technology, medicine etc.) and former non-academic programmes (e.g. preschool teachers, nurses etc). Thus, traditional Swedish higher education comprises the programmes and discipline areas that were described as higher education prior to the reform of 1977.

a straight line. Rather there have been strong variations for different groups over different periods. Figure 3:2 below shows that all groups decreased

**Figure 3:2**   New enrolments, 1 000 (After SCB, 1980, p. 59)

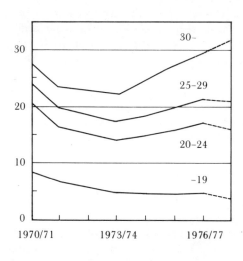

**Figure 3:1** Age-distribution in Swedish higher education from 1900-1980. (Source *UHÄ-rapport 1982:17*, page 14)

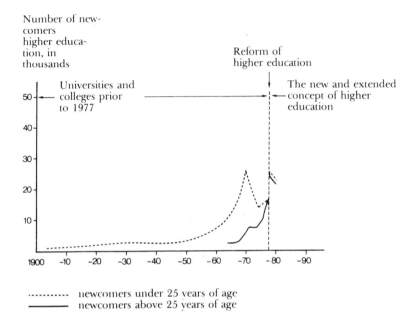

...... newcomers under 25 years of age
——— newcomers above 25 years of age

in the early seventies, while older students increased and young students decreased in the mid-seventies prior to the reform of 1977. In 1983 this tendency has changed. The number of young applicants has again increased substantially, while the number of adults has stabilized or in some study programmes seen a slight decrease.[1]

A publication of the National Bureau of Statistics (SBC, 1983) compares the level of adult participation 1978 and 1981. Table 3:2 (page 18) presents the number of registered students in higher education on graduate level by age.[2] The percentage of registered students of 25 years of age or older has increased slowly since 1978 (57%), 1979 (59%), 1980 (61%), and 1981 (62%). A major part of the adult students still study separate courses. These figures include all kinds of students, both general degree-oriented programmes and students enrolled in separate courses.

NBUC has recently published a report on the age distribution of new enrolments of the academic year of 1982/83:[3] (table 3:3, page 18)

**Table 3:2**  Age distribution and total number of students in 1978 and 1981

| Autumn term | Age at the end of the year | | | | | | | | Sum. | Total |
|---|---|---|---|---|---|---|---|---|---|---|
| | -19 | 20-24 | 25-29 | 30-34 | 35-39 | 40-44 | 45-54 | -55 | | |
| 1978 | 4 | 39 | 23 | 14 | 8 | 5 | 5 | 2 | 100 | 157,000 |
| 1981 | 3 | 35 | 24 | 14 | 11 | 6 | 5 | 2 | 100 | 159,000 |

**Table 3:3**  Age distribution among newcomers 1982/83 – an overview

| | Age groups (%) | | | |
|---|---|---|---|---|
| | -21 | 22-24 | 25-34 | 35- |
| *Degree programmes* | | | | |
| The four big univ | 31 | 20 | 27 | 22 |
| | 31 | 20 | 27 | 22 |
| Other univ and advanced colleges | 30 | 19 | 28 | 23 |
| Regional colleges | 30 | 15 | 25 | 30 |
| Municipal higher education | 19 | 14 | 41 | 26 |
| Total figure | 29 | 18 | 29 | 24 |
| *Separate courses* | | | | |
| The four big univ | 28 | 18 | 26 | 28 |
| | 25 | 17 | 28 | 30 |
| Other adv. colleges | 13 | 12 | 32 | 43 |
| Regional colleges | 16 | 10 | 27 | 47 |
| Municipal higher education | - | 2 | 36 | 62 |
| Total figure | 22 | 14 | 28 | 36 |

Source UHÄ (1985), page 18

The result shows that separate courses recruit adult students more often than degree programmes. Further, regionally situated colleges and municipal higher education have more adult students than traditional universities or advanced schools of professional education, e.g. in the field of technology.

*Trends in different educational sectors*
The number of adult students varies between different educational sectors. Young students, i.e. students younger than 25 years, are in the majority in two sectors (programmes of advanced technology and programmes in the field of administrative, economic and social professions:[4]

**Figure 3:3**   Percentage of students younger than 25 years (1978 and 1981).

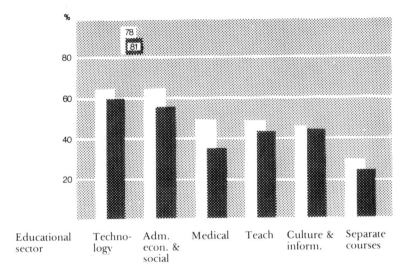

Adult participation is dependent on our criterion of assessment. Newly enrolled students tend to be younger than the total student population. Thus, the median age of the total student population for autumn 1980 was 26 years, compared to 24 years for newly enrolled students. The average age (median) of newly enrolled students both in general degree-oriented programmes and separate courses is illustrated by the table below.[5]

**Table 3:4**   Median age of newly enrolled students in different sectors and in the field of separate courses
Source   *SCB (1983)*

|  | Median age of newly enrolled students | | | |
|---|---|---|---|---|
| *Educational sector* | 1977/78 | 1978/79 | 1979/80 | 1980/81 |
| Technical occupations | 20 | 21 | 21 | 21 |
| Administrative, economic and social occupations | 21 | 21 | 21 | 21 |
| Medical and paramedical professions | 23 | 24 | 24 | 25 |
| Teaching profession | 22 | 24 | 24 | 23 |
| Culture and information | 22 | 22 | 22 | 22 |
| Separate courses | 27 | 28 | 28 | 27 |
| The total system | 24 | 24 | 24 | 24 |

The median age of the total student population is 24 years. It is easy to see the strong influence of the separate courses of the adultification process.

Women are in the majority in the total student population, but heavily underrepresented in certain sectors; e.g. programmes of advanced technology. The age/sex distribution of 1980 is given in figure 3:4 (page 21).[6]

## Difficult to describe part-time students

It is difficult to give a current picture of the number of part-time students in Sweden. The explanation is partly a technical one, because the concept of part-time student is not used in common higher education statistics. Partly it depends on the fact that few special surveys on study patterns were done in the early eighties. We know, however, that the new students developed another study pattern than conventional students. This phenomenon was reflected in the NBUC budget proposal for the fiscal year of 1975/76 (written in 1974):

> Within faculties of the humanities and natural sciences, a new pattern of studies has emerged in recent years. Similar tendencies are probably also to be expected within other faculties. This new pattern

**Figure 3:4**   Autumn term 1980, 158 280 registered students.

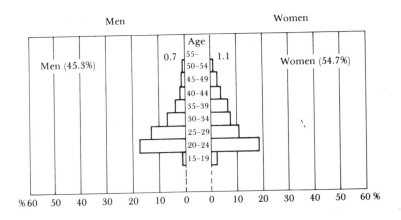

of studies is characterized not only by an ongoing decline in the number of students opting for general study programmes but also by the increasing number who are interested in shorter study programmes and in evening and part-time studies

NBUC budget proposal
UHÄ-rapport 1974:20, page 18

The statistics for the first half of 1970 showed a marked increase in interest in part-time studies. We also know that part-time studies correlate with age. In the mid-seventies NBUC conducted a special survey on part-time students at the faculties of arts and sciences. The study was not wholly representative of all students at this faculty. It is interesting to see, however, the strong correlation between age and part-time studies (table 3:5, page 22).[7]

As has been mentioned above there is also a strong relation between age and occupational activity. The table below emanates from the same survey. 59% of the sample mentioned work as their main activity during the spring of 1975, while the corresponding figure for studies was 33%. If we relate age to main activity, we obtain the following result: (table 3:6, page 22)

## The adultification and the 25:4-scheme

'Adultification' cannot be explained by the 25:4-scheme (see appendix 2 for further explanation). The table below shows the educational background of

21

**Table 3:5**  Study pattern and age
**Source**  *NBUC (1976)*

| Age | Normal study rate | Part-time | Total |
|---|---|---|---|
| -24 | 485 (50%) | 482 (50%) | 967 (100%) |
| 25-44 | 369 (22%) | 1316 (78%) | 1685 (100%) |
| 45- | 32 (11%) | 262 (89%) | 294 (100%) |
| Total | 886 (30%) | 2060 (70%) | 2946 (100%) |

Information not available 1%

**Table 3:6**  Age and main activity
**Source**  *NBUC (1976)*

| | Age | | | |
|---|---|---|---|---|
| *Main activity* | -24 | 25-44 | 45- | Total |
| Gainfully employed | 257 ( 27%) | 1233 ( 74%) | 242 ( 83%) | 1732 |
| Student | 642 ( 67%) | 309 ( 18%) | 26 ( 9%) | 977 |
| Other | 64 ( 7%) | 133 ( 8%) | 25 ( 9%) | 222 |
| Total | 936 (100%) | 1675 (100%) | 293 (100%) | 2931 |

Information not available 2%

students admitted to general study programmes. 25:4-students make up about 5% of enrolments in general study programmes, while they comprise almost 50% of enrolments in separate courses. Another complication is that only 50% of the 25:4 scheme students can be labelled as 'genuine 25:4-students'. The other 50% are students who, for technical reasons, are admitted as 25:4-scheme students, but who also could apply in other access channels (table 3:7, page 23).[8]

The rise in the number of adult students was due partly to the introduction of the 25:5 rule and also to the gradual adjustment of the range of courses to suit new groups of students: part-time evening courses,

**Table 3:7** Educational background of students admitted to general study programmes

Source *SCB (1983)*

| Year | 3-4 years upper secondary scholary | 2 years upper secondary scholary | Other eligible education | 25:4 Exception from adm. rules | Excep- tion from adm. rules | Foreign educa- tion | Folk high school | Un- known educa- tion | Total |
|---|---|---|---|---|---|---|---|---|---|
| 1977/78 | 7,803 | 1,712 | 215 | 494 | 109 | 776 | 233 | 660 | 12,002 |
| 1978/79 | 8,478 | 2,186 | 221 | 692 | 52 | 846 | 320 | 637 | 13,432 |
| 1979/80 | 7,949 | 2,225 | 244 | 654 | 49 | 533 | 298 | 666 | 12,618 |
| 1980/81 | 8,477 | 5,008 | 242 | 726 | 51 | 518 | 398 | 993 | 16,413 |

distance teaching and short-cycle courses. For example, in the academic year of 1969/70 there were only about ten courses at the faculties of arts and sciences carrying 10 credits or less. The corresponding figure in the academic year 1976/77 was about 200. Further, distance education and off-campus provision of higher education contributed to the new study pattern.[9]

First-time enrolments under the 25:5 rule in the 1976/77 academic year accounted for almost a quarter of all first-time enrolments at the liberal arts faculties, compared with just over 9 per cent in 1971/72. The same period also witnessed a steep rise in the number of enrolled students exempted from the general requirements of admission: over 15 per cent of first-time enrolments at liberal arts faculties in 1976/77 as against 4-5 per cent in 1971/72. This development is also described by Kim (1982) in her case study on the Swedish 25:5-scheme (table 3:8, page 24).

Within the faculties of arts and sciences the dramatic changes took place prior to the higher education reform, while other areas of university and post-secondary education were not affected more noticeably until after 1977. The higher education reform, however, was followed by a distinct rise in the average age of students enrolled in certain programmes for which there were large numbers of applicants; see table 3:9 (page 24).[10]

It is interesting to note that students of law and dental studies are still younger than 25. The reasons underlying the increase in the number of law students require further analysis.

Medical students are always an interesting policy example. In the academic year 1976/77, 65 per cent of students embarking on these studies

**Table 3:8**   New entrants to the liberal arts faculties 1969-1976
Source   Kim(1982)

| | New entrants in the year | | | | | | |
|---|---|---|---|---|---|---|---|
| Eligibility | 1969/70 | 70/71 | 71/72 | 72/73 | 73/74 | 74/75 | 75/76 |
| Admitted by the 25:5 rule | 4,8 | 6,4 | 8,3 | 11,0 | 15,2 | 19,8 | 22,5 |
| Admitted by exemption | 4,1 | 4,2 | 4,0 | 5,4 | 6,9 | 12,6 | 12,1 |
| 'Normal' eligibility (or un-known) | 91,1 | 89,4 | 87,7 | 83,6 | 77,9 | 67,6 | 65,4 |
| Total | 100,0 | 100,0 | 100,0 | 100,0 | 100,0 | 100,0 | 100,0 |
| (Total number of students) | (24055) | (22938) | (18105) | (18171) | (17321) | (19545) | (22002) |

**Table 3:9**  Proportion of beginners under 25 enrolled in various higher education programmes
Source   *SBC (1980)* p. 63

| Programme | 1972/73 | 1976/77 | aut. term 1977 | aut. term 1978 |
|---|---|---|---|---|
| Medical studies | 76,5 | 65,7 | 34,6 | 31,6 |
| Dental studies | 81,6 | 79,2 | 56,8 | 60,5 |
| Law | 64,4 | 62,1 | 68,2 | 70,2 |
| Social work and public administration | 62,1 | 58,3 | 45,7 | 42,3 |
| Pre-school teacher training | 71,6 | 66,2 | 58,4 | 49,2 |
| Junior level teacher training | 86,5 | 84,2 | 43,1 | 42,2 |
| Intermediate level teacher training | 81,1 | 79,8 | 50,7 | 44,1 |
| Nursing | 80,9 | 74,7 | 51,7 | 43,4 |

were 24 years old or younger. In the autumn term of 1977 – the first term after the reform – this figure fell to about 25 per cent, and in the autumn term of 1978 it was barely 32 per cent. Almost 40 per cent of newly enrolled medical students were 30 years old or more. A similar trend is displayed in junior and intermediate level teacher training and in dental studies, though the last mentioned reverted almost to 'normal' in the autumn term of 1978. The increasing age of medical students has been exaggerated in the public debate. In 1980/81, 60% of the students were below 25 years of age, 35% between 25-34 years of age and only 5% were older than 35. Thus the increasing age was stabilized or even decreased somewhat in this field.

The reason for the distinct changes following the reform of higher education can be found in the new rules of access, particularly those concerning the evaluation of qualifications. The introduction of credits for job experience meant a new chance for adults who had previously been excluded from the studies of their first preference.

## Adult higher education as part of general educational policy

From a more general policy perspective, increased adult participation can be seen as one indicator of the post-war broadening of higher education in Sweden. It also forms an important step in the development from elite higher education to mass higher education. At the end of the fifties, only 5-6 per cent of an 'age group' were matriculated in upper secondary school. Today, almost 25 years later, as many as 85-90 per cent of the 'age group' will participate in upper secondary schooling, and more than 50 per cent meet the general requirements for higher education (Kim, 1983). The educational capacity of the upper secondary school system was extended during the sixties, thereby increasing the total number of places in the system of upper secondary schools. The strongest increase has taken place within the vocational programmes while the theoretical study programmes have been unaffected or even seen a slight decrease. The number of students making the transition from the gymnasium to higher education rose somewhat compared to the fifties (when 60-70 per cent of the students went on to higher education). The enrolments of adults over 25 years of age showed a growing trend, but were still at a low level.

At the beginning of the seventies, Sweden like many other western countries, was struck by the declining enrolment of young students to higher education. Thus the decreasing interest in higher studies among the younger generation and a free sector of educational opportunities in the faculties of arts and sciences, happened to be beneficial and timely for the older generation. The Swedish Open Door policy and the experiment with the 25:5-scheme facilitated the increasing enrolment of adult students. The provision of new vocationally oriented short courses met the new study pattern with part-time studies, evening classes and a decreasing 'degree-orientation' among the students. At the end of the seventies the balance between young and old students changed once more. The new admission system in the reformed organization of higher education opened the doors even more for the working population and also for students of two year programmes in upper secondary schools. Parallel to this development, the Swedish Riksdag took a decision in 1979 to plan and control the educational capacity of higher education by implementing a numerus clausus. The result was not only a raised level of competition and conflicts between young and adult students in the admission game, but also a new debate about the risk that an 'adultification' of higher education was becoming too expensive.

The number of applicants to restricted programmes has almost trebled from the reform year 1977 to 1982 (from 20 900 to 55 500). In spite of modifications in the admission system aiming at better opportunities for students coming directly from upper secondary schools (less relative weight for work experience and more places for direct students), there has been a decrease in the relative proportion of students up to 20 years who have been admitted. This development is well known to the government, which has presented a plan for 23 000 new student places during the eighties '... in order to give the increasing population of young students the same educational opportunities - relatively speaking - as the population of young students during the seventies ...' As Kim (1983) shows, it is not easy to operationalize the concept 'the same educational opportunities of young students in the seventies ...' Irrespective of the vagueness of the policy definitions, it is quite evident that the balance between young and adult students is a crucial policy problem in Swedish higher education during the current decade and it will certainly be so in the 1990s.[11]

We have earlier used the concept 'adultification' of Swedish higher education i.e. that the majority of students are above 25 years of age. The meaning of this statement has to be specified. Firstly, it is necessary to distinguish on the one hand between 'newcomers' entering the system for the first time and, on the other, the student population already present in the system of higher education. Secondly, and this is a distinction of special value in the current OECD study, we have to divide the student population into students in general degree-oriented programmes and students in separate courses. Thirdly, we could analyze enrolment pattern and student population in one of the five different educational sectors of Swedish higher education. Finally, we could compare institutions of higher education of different sizes and regional functions.

26

# The process of 'adultification' – a concluding remark

Thus, there are different criteria to be used if we want to analyze the realities behind the concept of 'adultification'. The purpose of this book is not to give a final and definitive answer, but to present some statistical illustrations and policy trends on the themes mentioned above. The first part of this study can be summarized in the following points:

• Adult students are more often found in separate courses than degree oriented programmes.
• Younger students are more often found in the sector of technological professions and in the sector of administrative, economic and social professions.
• Students with a vocational background have more often been recruited to medium-size or small higher education institutions than at big universities and advanced colleges.
• The 'adultification' of Swedish higher education can only to a minor extent be explained by adult students embarking on the 25:4 scheme. Genuine 25:4 students are about 5% in general programmes, but almost 50% in separate courses.
• In general one could say that 'adultification' is a long-term process with roots going back to the late fifties. The reform of 1977 is an adaptation to a long term pattern. Further it is necessary to underscore that the reform of 1977 has been implemented parallel to the discontinuation of the old educational regulation of 1969. The new students can also be characterized by a new study pattern: more part-time, more evening classes and decreasing degree-orientation.
• Despite a national policy of reaching better balance between young students and adults (by giving 'direct' students better opportunities) the percentage of adult students has increased between 1978 and 1981.

# 4    Adults in degree-oriented programmes – trends and examples

## Programme structure and curriculum development for adults

From a policy point of view, it is important to analyze and discuss the educational consequences of the 'adultification' of Swedish higher education. To what extent do institutions of higher education adapt to the new study pattern with more part-time studies, evening classes, distance education and less degree-orientation? Are adult students a relatively homogeneous group? Is it possible to design a special curriculum for adults? These questions are vital if we want to discuss adult participation in degree-programmes.

The Swedish higher education system incorporates over 130 general study programmes in 23 localities. The selection of programmes ranges from a number of short-term and previously non-academic programmes to more long-term professional programmes taking four or five years to complete. The most professionally oriented programmes seem to come within the sector in which scientific specialization is most advanced, i.e. medicine and technology. Medicine and dentistry, pharmacology, degree studies in engineering and degree studies in architecture are common examples. Within these fields there is also a well-defined labour market with definite professional roles and a definite job structure.

These conditions do not apply to the same extent to some of the programmes within the traditional university field such as the faculties of arts and science. As has been mentioned above, the concept of general study programme is a crucial part of the reform. The idea of a core curriculum emanates from programmes in technology and medicine, and it has not been easy to transform it for the use in the traditional higher education subjects. Many of the difficulties in designing effective study programmes in some areas in the humanities are still unsolved.

The distribution of new enrolments in programmes of various lengths in the academic year 1978/79 was as follows:

**Figure 4:1**  An overview of the programme structure with regard to programme length.

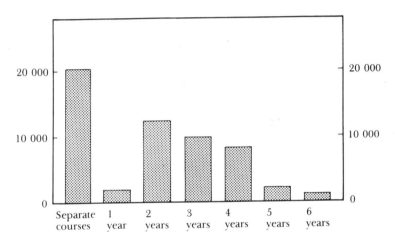

Besides the separate courses, 2, 3 and 4-year programmes are the most common ones in the system.[1] The majority of these programmes, independently of programme length, are provided both for young and adult students. The trend towards integrated programmes has been strong in Swedish higher education policy. There are only a few examples of shortened programmes for working adults. In fact in some areas such as medicine, health, and pre-school-teaching existing shortened programmes have been eliminated in favour of integrated programmes.

A bid to renew and establish wide educational programmes can be seen in the report of a NBUC task force on the structure of programmes within the sector of Administrative, Economic, and Social Education. This task force proposed that the existing nine programmes be reduced to three. The Swedish Riksdag (Parliament) decided to approve ths curriculum reform during spring 1983. The new set of general programmes was built on a principle of successive differentiation, i.e. more fundamental subjects in the first two years and possibilities to specialize later on.

One exception to this rule of programme integration is the experiment with shorter vocational programmes for technicians (YTH). This experimental schedule started in 1975 as a result of a proposal from the U 68 commission. The purpose was

- to meet the needs of higher education of an underprivileged group,
- to meet the industrial demand for professional up-grading of technicians,
- to contribute to the training of vocational teachers.

The programmes were designed for adults with a professionally relevant experience. The evaluation of this experiment has shown that it has been successful in relation to the above specified goals. Löfgren has recently presented a study of career-related utilization of the YTH-programme.[2] He found that more than two of three students were engaged in more qualified tasks or changed jobs / positions one year after the completion of their studies.

Another example is a shortened programme for nurses aiming to become medical doctors. Experiences in this field have not been as positive as with the YTH-programme. The Caroline Institute of Medicine recommended that the NBUC eliminate this programme. In one of the last Government Bills of Education a decision was taken to cut the programme, but to give nurses increasing opportunities to study in regular programmes of medicine.[3]

Our knowledge of the developments of individual study programmes and local programmes is limited. We know that the possibility of developing individual programmes is seldom used. A more interesting aspect, seen from the point of view of innovation in higher education, is local programmes.

As has been mentioned above, it is the regional boards which have specific responsibility to support the development of local study programmes. It would be interesting to clarify to what extent these boards have had the capacity to meet this challenge.

## The idea of phased exits in degree-programmes

One important feature of the Swedish planning strategy for recurrent education is the division of longer study programmes into phased exits. This, however, has involved great difficulties and has so far only been applied in a few of the traditional sectors in the universities and colleges e.g.

legal training. Another example is provided by the arrangement enabling childminders to build on their previous training in order to qualify as pre-school teachers. It has not been possible to divide some of the longer professional programmes (e.g. advanced technology, medicine or pharmacy) into parts or modules. The idea has been successful, however, where other medical and paramedical programmes are concerned; i.e. in that part of the Swedish system of higher education which is the shared responsibility of the state and the County Councils. Phased exits differ from traditional short-cycle higher education, which has been built up to provide short-term courses regarded as self-contained units, and not in accordance with the principle of phased exits.[4]

The possibilities of arranging phased exits are partly dependent on subject structure, interdisciplinary relations and sequencing. The more powerful the structural links between the various parts of a course of education, the more difficult it will be to arrange phasing without impeding the growth of the student's cognitive structure. The well-known difficulty entailed by phasing is that of integrating demands for education to lead to both horizontal and vertical mobility in the labour market. If broad initial education is provided, this will lead to better opportunities for horizontal mobility but not for vertical mobility. It is hard to reconcile the demand that each phase constitutes a complete course of vocational training with the demand for a wide education in which the definitive vocational training comes as late as possible.

It follows that the feasibility of phased exits varies between the five sectors of the higher education system. The present account will be confined to the labour market aspect. Phased exits are based on the premise that there is space in the labour market for persons who have undergone this type of training, i.e. training in which every stage leads to a clearly defined vocational level. Thus the advocates of phased exits in a given sector mainain that job echelons in the sector are distributed in such a way that there would be scope for graduates with the structure of qualifications concerned. The opponents of these ideas believe, to put things simply, that there is no need for 'semi-graduates'.

In view of the importance attached to the question of phased exits in the reform process, it is interesting to analyse the failure of implementing this idea. One explanation is of course, the shortage of financial resources. According to some opponents, phased exits would call for more resources and development of parallel programmes. Another contributory factor was that the concept of recurrent education was primarily a general model for alternation between education and employment. The concept itself did not indicate how it was to be applied to different education programmes.

Thus the idea of phased exits did not gain any strong support among professors and university teachers in general. Different arguments were raised against it, e.g. cognitive and organizational needs for keeping long-term professionally oriented study programmes together, financial and administrative costs for having two parallel programmes, and, also the difficulties in relating the shorter study programme to the occupational structure and demand for qualified labour.

The feasibility of phased exits should also be viewed in relation to the idea of a decentralized higher education system. The ultimate responsibility for educational plans and their determination of the scope of a programme rests with the central planning authority, NBUC. The task of the local programme boards was to invest education with form and content within the framework of the overriding principles. Most of the members of the programme boards are teachers and researchers.

Findings from the project entitled 'The adaptation of universities and colleges to recurrent education' indicate that certain programme boards take the view that general study programmes are mainly intended for young students and that the increased resources channelled into this form of education imply a definite allocation of priority to young students. Many planners saw an antithesis between programme studies and adult education and maintain that individual courses exist to cater for the educational needs of adults.[5]

When the idea of recurrent education was propounded in connection with the reform of higher education, the Minister of Education at that time stated: 'I anticipate that recurrent education – as a pattern for the utilization of the educational machinery – will gradually become a realistic alternative to the present order of things, which is primarily based on continuous education during childhood and adolescence'.[6] This statement reflects the uncertainty of Government and Riksdag concerning the speed at which recurrent education was to evolve and concerning the price at which this was to be accomplished. The vagueness with which recurrent education was talked about made it possible to disregard the difficult questions concerning the establishment of priorities.

Thus the idea of phased exits has not been successfully implemented. Another problem area relating to general study programmes is that a majority of students in the traditional faculties of arts and sciences prefer to study separate courses instead of degree-programmes. In spite of the reform of 1977, which involved a new system of curricula, students take the traditional university subjects under the cover name of separate courses.

## Study results and drop-out rates

Another policy issue in Sweden concerns how efficient the higher education system is regarding the rate of graduation. One investigation at the university of Lund provides empirical evidence showing that the study results in the new system have not – as far as the university of Lund is concerned – been better than under the 1969 educational regulation. Contradictory evidence, has been published by Bladh in a broad survey of the trends in the Swedish programme structure.[7] Her reports are the main sources for the description and analysis presented in the following paragraphs.

Special attention has been paid to nine general and degree-oriented study programmes, (physics, chemistry, mathematics, system approaches and computers, economics, social science, psychology, teaching and so called cultural knowledge). Before going into statistical details, Bladh spends much time in analyzing the difficulties of interpreting and using different sources of Swedish statistics. It is not an exaggeration to say that a main part of the discussion of reform evaluation in Sweden from 1977 onwards has been concerned with the obstacles and solutions to finding a better system of statistical documentation of study patterns. One of the interesting parts in the report is an effort to compare study results of students taking programmes under the previous 1969 educational regulation and the new system. In contrast to the Lund study, Bladh finds that there is empirical evidence showing that the new system might be more efficient as far as study streams and study results are concerned. It is necessary to underscore, however, that these investigations concern students in general and not adults in particular.

In another part of Bladh's work a comparison is made between students of programmes in physics as contrasted to those in economics, with respect to drop-out levels. After four semesters 35% of the 'physicists' and 17% of the 'economists' had dropped out either temporarily or definitely. The higher drop-out level of the physics programme cannot be explained by age-factors, as the students in physics are much younger than those in economics. One must look instead into other factors such as curriculum content, forms of teaching and learning and the students' educational backgrounds, subject knowledge and, not least, motivation.

In comparison with the early seventies, we lack a comprehensive picture of drop-out rates and retention strategies in Swedish higher education. It is not only a problem of insufficient statistical documentation, but also a redefinition of the drop-out concept as such. The so called 'new study pattern' with more part-time and less degree-orientation does not necessarily have to be negative for society and working life. But who can judge if a 'drop-out' is good or bad? The increasing vagueness of the concept tends to be a policy problem in itself. Apart from this conceptual aspect of policy evaluation there is some evidence that different groups of adults face considerable study problems and social conflicts.[8]

## Adult students as 'resource persons'

The project 'work experience as a resource in higher education', which forms part of the reform evaluation programme at the NBUC, has tried to analyze the concept of work experience in relation to different knowledge definitions in three higher education programmes (physicists, teacher training and nursing). One of the main results of this project is that work experience has different resource values in different programmes. Life and work experience are more beneficial in 'soft-science-programmes' such as teacher education and nurses training than in technology and science. Furthermore, this evaluation supported the conclusions, generated within a previous study by Abrahamsson, Kim and Rubenson, who analyzed work experience as a substitute for formal academic knowledge.[9]

Life and work experience is not a study skill in itself, but it adds important perspectives and frames of references, which can have a mirror-function in interpreting academic knowledge. In spite of this resource aspect, there is evidence that students with a 25:4-scheme background may encounter difficulties in the most theoretical study programmes. These study problems not only reflect cognitive aspects and subject knowledge, but also the effects of more restricted time-budgets as a function of family obligations.

Looking at study statistics and drop-out rates it is necessary to keep two things in mind. Firstly, we must once more underline the fact that the group of adult students is very heterogeneous where social, financial and cultural aspects are concerned. Secondly, we must not forget that study problems and drop-out rates can also be high for young students. Furthermore, we must clarify the differences in educational context between different sectors of Swedish higher education and between general programmes and separate courses.

## Adults at degree-level – some conclusions

The current Swedish trend of adult higher education where degree studies are concerned could be summarized in the following way:

• the policy stresses the need for integrated programmes characterized by a balance between theoretical knowledge and practical training, scientific perspectives and working life issues.

• the policy of curricula-integration comprises few experiments with programmes designed for working adults. There are, however, some interesting exceptions (YTH, shortened programmes for nurses and pre-school teachers...). The North American idea of recognizing prior learning (RPL) is used very seldom. An adult student with significant professional experience might meet bureaucratic obstacles if he or she wants to have this experience recognized as a substitute for course studies.

• the curriculum development goes from individualization to integration. Individual study programmes are seldom used. Local study programmes as well as general study programmes are adaptations to students' needs on a collective level, not on an individual level.

• work experience is mainly used as an admission merit and not as a professional competence or study skill as such. The utilization of prior life and work experiences varies from programme to programme depending on curricular content, programme design, composition of student population.

• we know that adults admitted on the basis of work experience have difficulties in some professionally oriented programmes, especially in the field of advanced technology, where the drop-out rates are high. On the other hand, they are successful in other programmes, which offer better possibilities to use their prior experiences and competence. If we want to analyze how successful adult students are in Swedish higher education it is necessary to specify our criteria of successful educational condition and relevant groups of comparison.

• the question whether adult students are more successful than young students cannot be answered with a simple yes or a no. Adults in Swedish higher education comprise a variety of students with different social, educational, economic and occupational background. The so called 25:4-scheme students are far fewer than 10% in degree programmes and almost 50% in separate courses. In general one could say that adult students have more motivation and experiences, but a more restricted life situation and time budget compared to younger students.

• the idea of a specific curriculum for adult higher education has not been developed in Sweden. Rather, the adult student is integrated in programmes open for all kinds of students.

• the last years, there has been a public debate on the qualification value of subject marks of municipal adult education, especially what studies at upper secondary level is concerned. In order to compare the performance of adults and young students, the Swedish National Board of Education has taken an initiative to a comparative study on the following three subjects; Swedish, English and mathematics.

• as a consequence of this debate and other considerations, the Swedish admission commission has raised the idea of general entrance tests for adults.

# 5   Adults in continuing higher education – trends and examples

## What is continuing higher education?

In a comparative perspective it is important to make a distinction between credit and non-credit higher education. When we describe the phenomenon 'continuing higher education' we include both credit and non-credit courses. Thus, the notion of continuing higher education in Sweden comprises a variety of educational realities, which can be sorted into the following main categories:

a separate courses as a part of the 1977 programme structure
b extramural higher education according to the idea of university circles provided by the independent study associations
c commissioned higher education courses, where the employers or other societal agents pay for cooperative educational measures
d higher learning as staff development and in-service training within the public or private sector.

Another distinction goes between campus and off-campus higher education. Continuing higher education could also be described in the context of different forms of knowledge dissemination, e.g. distance education, decentralized courses and other measures to provide educational opportunities as close as possible to the students' life and work setting.

Higher education as a part of further and continuing education has high priority in Sweden if one is to believe official statements. The Government's

Bill of Finance regarding the educational sector of 1982/83:100 stresses this fact:

> The separate courses are mainly intended to provide subsequent and further education. About 70 per cent of these students are over 25 years old. I would like to emphasize that the ability of a higher education system to offer subsequent and further education and opportunities even for slightly older persons to take general study programmes has an important bearing on the development of the economy in the public sector and also on the ability of the economically active to assert themselves in a changing labour market. The pace of technical progress is now very rapid. This is transforming production processes and job content with them. Similar effects are also being produced in the public sector, for example in public administration and in medical care. In order to accomplish successfully the structural changes that are needed in industry and the public sector, we will have to provide scope for subsequent and further education. Needs of this kind are in fact more pressing today than when preparations were being made for the reform of the higher education system. This makes it essential, even during the years with large generations of young persons of university age, to pay attention to the balance between the various educational tasks of the higher education system and the balance between young and mature students.
>
> Government Bill of Education 1982/83, page 376

In practice, however, some recent budget cuts have, up to 1984, been more common in the field of separate courses than in general degree-oriented programmes, which partly is due to the increased 'youth-orientation' in Swedish higher education in the shift between the 1970s and 1980s. In the Bill of Finance of 1984, the balance between youth education and adult education is somewhat restored in relation to the reform ideals. NBUC has been discussing this problem in a rather recent budget proposal to the government.[1] Budget cuts among separate courses tend to have severe consequences for small subjects within the traditional faculties of arts and sciences. Another main policy problem is to find methods of reallocating resources within separate courses. The development of new courses in the area of technology, economy and administration is very expensive. The possibilities of providing 'fresh' money from the national government are limited and in order to create one new course one has to eliminate at least one or maybe two or three old courses.

The rapid technological development and the changes of the working life structure from the production of commodities to the development of knowledge systems is an enormous challenge to continuing higher education. The formal system of higher education is more or less voluntarily taking part in a 'knowledge race' with different non-formal ways of facilitating higher learning. If our institutions of higher education are not capable of providing qualified knowledge in this development, the big enterprises and organizations will take the initiative instead. Thus, a more general discussion of continuing higher education must incorporate a broad scope of learning environments of both intramural and extramural character. The discussion in this chapter will, however, mainly concern the first two forms of continuing higher education in Sweden. Commissioned higher education is increasing, but we still lack a comprehensive picture of its development. The schools of advanced technology seem to be active in this field as are small or medium-size colleges operating on a regional level.[2]

## Problems in the area of separate courses

The other main programme measure in the Swedish strategy of recurrent education was the concept of separate courses (enstaka kurser). Short-cycle courses had existed at unversities for a long time previously. Studies in the faculties of arts and science have traditionally been composed of various academic subjects and courses. In the new system, the separate course allocation has become an important part of the educational structure of Swedish higher education. A substantial portion of higher education takes the form of separate courses. In some sectors, particularly the sector of education for administrative, economic and social professions and the sector of education for cultural and information professions, the programmes cater for only part of the students' long-term educational demands.

But, on the other hand, the separate course allocation also has to finance other kinds of education within the higher education units. Statements made by the Government and Riksdag in various contexts before and after the reform of higher education point to a very wide range of uses. The purpose of separate courses can be summarized as follows:[3]

Separate courses are intended to enhance the accessibility of higher education:

- By catering to new groups of students.
- By being offered in new fields (e.g. technology, nursing and medical care and education).
- By being available outside the university and college localities.

Separate courses are mainly intended to cater to *educational needs* other than those which are provided for in the general educational programmes:

- By adding to the diversity of educational opportunities
- By providing different groups with the subsequent and further education they need.
- By being amenable to the organization and planning of recurrent education.
- By being provided for students with a more general educational interest.

How can we measure if the system of separate courses has been successful? In general, one could say that the reform aimed at a good and constructive balance between different aspects of higher education e.g. the balance between young students and adults and the balance between general study programmes and separate courses. It is no exaggeration to say that Swedish policy-makers and higher education planners experience a marked imbalance in the programme structure. The demand for short-cycle and separate courses is much stronger than the demand for general study programmes, and this especially holds for the traditional faculties of arts and science. Adult students, in particular, have requested separate courses. Recently it has been found that young students are also tending more and more to apply for separate courses.[4] Thus, students of all ages do not behave according to the intentions of the state or the general higher education policy.

But it is also true that a number of new course themes have been developed. Partly, this is due to the renewal of course content that took place in the early seventies, when the shorter vocationally oriented courses were introduced. Partly, it is a consequence of the new learners' increasing demands for shorter courses, suitable for part-time studies.

Thus, it is hard to say to what extent these changes are caused only by the reform as such, or if they are due to other developments in higher education or in society. However, it is obvious that the government wants to counteract this development by setting up a number of restrictions on the provision of separate courses. Consequently, a more austere interpretation of the scope and purpose of separate courses emerges from the 'Retrenchment Bill', which calls for a stricter review of amenities.[5] As an initial premise, short-cycle courses (less than 10 credits) of general introductory content which are not clearly distinguishable from popular education should be dispensed with. Short-term courses of a manifest in-depth or extension nature, and therefore normally conditional on previous higher studies, should not be affected by these economization measures (p. 20). 'At the same time, efforts should be made to improve the planning of individual courses in such a way that they can supplement one another in various fields as regards both the broadening and the deepening of studies' (p. 15).

The budget proposals of 1981 and onwards underline the importance of economization measures and better management of resources. Among other things, it is affirmed that previous statements in Government Bills concerning, for example, the renewal of education and recurrent education still hold 'albeit within more constricted economic frames. It is essential, in my opinion, that the work of renewal in higher education should not lose momentum' (p. 371 et seq.). The need for recurrent education is stressed once more. 'There will, in fact, be a greater need than ever for subsequent and further education within the higher system in order to facilitate transfers of labour between different parts of the public sector or from that sector to industry'.[6]

Ironically, the State is determined to restrict the range of separate courses of more general educational interest at the same time as the special subsidies for university circles run by the adult education associations are being removed, partly on the grounds that education of this kind is provided by the higher education system.

A study by Bladh provides further empirical evidence concerning study patterns in the sector of separate courses.[7] Between 1977 and 1979, prior to the decision on numerus clausus, the students applied for separate courses in the same manner as they had earlier taken subject-courses at the traditional faculties of arts and sciences. Further follow-up studies by SCB (the National Bureau of Statistics) point to the fact that very few students of separate courses continue for a full degree. Bladh comes to the conclusion that separate courses have not been a substitute for general study programmes. The usual pattern is to choose shorter courses in different subjects rather than to pursue further studies in one or two subjects.

Another interesting part of Bladh's study provides an account of the students' arguments for choosing separate courses (table 5:1, page 42).

This table can be interpreted in at least two ways. Firstly, it fits well with the discussion in the previous section on the increasing vocational interest among students at smaller institutions of higher education. Secondly, it illustrates the thesis presented by Bladh that students of separate courses at the traditional faculties of arts and sciences keep to their 'old study pattern', i.e. they prefer to develop themselves in an area of liberal education, while the state wants them to be more vocationally oriented. This tendency is even stronger when the students are asked about the subjective image of the use of their studies of separate courses, where 55% stated that separate courses increased their general knowledge and only 11% mentioned job-related uses. Thus, the majority of the students perceive general education to be the

**Table 5:1**  Comparison between motives for studying a separate course at bigger universities and other colleges (mainly medium size or small institutions of higher learning with regional functions
Source   Bladh (1983)

|  | *Universities* | *Other colleges* |
|---|---|---|
| Further training & skill upp-grading | 26 | 43 |
| Instead of gen. programme | 4 | 1 |
| Testing own's study capacity | 4 | 3 |
| Subject-interest | 33 | 27 |
| Need for credentials | 6 | 7 |
| Other         8 | 5 | |
| Partial drop-out | 19 | 14 |
|  | 100% | 100% |
|  | (9 838) | (5 112) |

primary function of the separate courses they take. Professional utilization tends to increase with age, but it does not receive nearly as much weight as the broader knowledge function.

The studies by Bladh provide important empirical data for a policy debate on the objectives and impact of the new programme structure in the Swedish system of higher education. The two main instruments are still general degree-oriented programmes and separate courses. The degree-programmes seem to function well in their traditional fields, e.g. technology and medicine, while there have been different obstacles to implement them in the fields of the traditional faculties of arts and science. In these fields, traditional subject studies are provided through the assumed name of separate courses.

Another important observation is that students of separate courses seldom go deeper into one or two subjects or continue to take a degree. The idea of recognizing prior learning and thereby adding the necessary subject courses is not used in Sweden. We have also very few examples of individual study programmes. If we look for innovations of this nature in the Swedish programme structure, it might be of interest to analyze the developments of new local study programmes.

## The Swedish model of distance education

The Swedish experiments with distance education form a part of the development work proposed by the U 68 commission on education. This proposal was a reflection of the U 68 ambition to find new ways of disseminating higher education. In the mid-seventies the Committee for Television and Radio in Education was given the task of proposing general models for the organization of distance education in Sweden. The committee presented different organizational models, partly inspired by the British Open University[8]. These proposals were neglected in the reform process and distance education was made an ordinary duty of each department of higher education in Sweden. The reform decision and the localization of higher education to new cities eliminated the need for a separate distance education system. As has been mentioned in the first section, distance education in Sweden is coordinated by the six regional boards as a part of their governmental support for separate courses.

The six regional boards have had an informal working group which is responsible for policy development and empirical investigations on the matter of distance education. The group published a policy-oriented report at the beginning of the autumn 1983.[9] During the academic year 82/83 244 distance courses were provided by Swedish universities and colleges. This represents about 6 000 new student places or about 2 500 full-time equivalents. In total, this means somewhat more than 6% of the total full-time student equivalents are channelled through distance education within the system of separate courses. The distribution among the regions is surprisingly uneven: (table 5:2, page 44)

Distance courses are provided in most subjects and the most common length is a one semester course (20 points). Of the 244 distance courses the variations are the following: 5 points (24), 10 points (87), 20 points (131), 40 points (1), 60 points (1). There are also one or two examples of general study programmes offered through distance education, but the common pattern is that distance courses mainly comprise short-cycle higher education and separate courses.

The development of Swedish distance education has been a subject of both policy and research interest for Dahllöf and Willén.[10] Distance education cannot, in their opinion, be analyzed as an instruction method per se. It has to be seen as part of a more integrated and flexible educational design; i.e. an adjustment to the new study pattern that developed in the

Table 5:2

| Region | % |
| --- | --- |
| Stockholm | 1,9 |
| Uppsala | 7,5 |
| Linköping | 12,4 |
| Lund/Malmö | 9,6 |
| Göteborg | 2,8 |
| Umeå | 18,9 |
| In total | 6,4 |

early seventies (more part-time, more evening studies and shorter study programmes). The regional boards have a crucial function in this adaptation process.

Distance education is, however, still a limited part of separate courses (about 6%) and almost totally absent in degree-studies. One explanation explanation, of course, is that the geographical availability of higher education has increased significantly during the seventies. We must not forget, however, that distance education is not only an answer to geographical isolation. It could also be used to meet the needs of adult students who cannot follow the regular programme schedules.

## Trends in extramural higher education and university circles

Another form of continuing higher education comprises the extramural courses, which have roots back to the late 19th century and the British University Extension movement. The administrative form of extramural higher education has been the university circle, which has had financial support from the government since 1945. NBE (National Board of Education) regulations stipulate that university circles must 'be conducted on essentially the same level as in universities and colleges. On the other hand, they need not adhere to the subjects or syllabi included in instruction at universities and colleges'. The regulations also stipulate special qualifications for the teacher, in principle the same as for other post-secondary teachers.[11]

How were the extramural university circles affected by the 1977 reform of higher education? The statistics show a gradual decline during the 1970s, beginning well before 1977. On the other hand non-curricular university circles rose steeply throughout the 70s. This increase, however, came to an abrupt halt the fiscal year 1981/82, when the total number of university circles fell from 3 656 in 1980/81 to 1 155. The explanation is simple. As from 1st July 1981, new regulations have come into force with respect to State grants allocated to university circles, whereby reduced grants are made towards circles held less than 30km away from university and college localities. In some cases this rule may have resulted in adult education associations receiving smaller grants for a circle classified as a university circle than the amount received for an ordinary study circle. In its final report, the latest Popular Education Commission considered the idea of abolishing university circles, but the Government and Riksdag decided to retain them. In practice, however, it seems that the concept of extramural university circles is disappearing as a consequence of the new financial stipulations.

During the seventies there has been an interesting development of new contacts and contracts between higher education, trade unions and the local community. Partly as a consequence of the policy interest in working life issues during the seventies a number of new courses were constructed, e.g. work environment, work legislation, administrative techniques etc. At some universities and colleges this new network has strongly stimulated curriculum development. The provision of societally oriented shorter courses at the university of Lund has led to a new concept, i.e. the 'research circle'.[12]

The idea behind the 'research circle' is that higher education is not only a tool of dissemination of prefabricated knowledge, but also an instrument of stimulating the working adults to do their own research on topics stemming from their job environment and local community. In order to facilitate this 'research process' post-graduate students have been used as resource persons in the courses. It is interesting to note that this 'radical' profile of higher education has developed within the separate courses of state higher education and not within the extramural higher education.

## Some concluding remarks

The future of Swedish continuing higher education is an open question. Economic stagnation and the restricted state budget influence the situation in two ways. On the one hand there is a growing need to meet the technological challenge for broader knowledge and skill-upgrading. On the other hand, the limited financial resources do not leave much room for innovations and development. More concretely, we can summarize:

- the field of separate courses is subject to budget cuts and re-allocation of resources
- the notion of separate courses has not functioned as a tool of professional up-grading, as a majority of students state that these courses have mainly given broader knowledge, which has not been useful in various work-situations.
- the roots of this problem can be traced back to problems in the traditional faculties of arts and science long before the reform, i.e. the notion of separate courses tends to be a new label for courses provided traditionally in social science and the humanities
- the need of distance education and a more flexible educational design will increase in a restricted budget situation
- the development of extramural higher education is full of contradiction. The idea of the university circle is disappearing, while a new concept of 'research circle' is created within a new pattern of contacts between universities and trade unions
- commissioned higher education tends to attract increasing policy attention, but we still have neither accurate statistics nor empirical evidence to describe the development in practice.
- the same goes for higher learning as an integrated part of staff development and in-service training. It is apparent however, that we meet a growing policy interest in this field both from the trade unions and from the state. And, this policy interest is now even stronger in the light of the government Bill on renewal funds, which was accepted by the Parliament in the end of 1984. These funds will be financed by 10% of the profits of the bigger enterprises, and they are mainly intended for research, development and training.

# 6 Higher education as part of adult education

## Traditions, objectives and structure in adult education

For several reasons, it is imperative that higher education be viewed in the context of adult education. Firstly, the idea of recurrent education comprises not only higher education, but a variety of institutions of formal education, where different organizers of adult education play important roles. Secondly, institutions of adult education, and especially municipal adult education and folk high schools (residential colleges for adults with a liberal education curriculum), are important recruitment channels for higher education. Adult students have to pursue subject-related studies in municipal adult education in order to meet the specific entrance requirements. Thirdly, there is a growing need to discuss the division of labour and organizational responsibilities between higher education and different institutions of adult education.[1]

Sweden has a long and enduring tradition of adult education. The first activities in this field go back to the late 18th century, when the Patriotic Society was transformed into the Society of Common Civic Knowledge.[2] The distribution of leaflets and other information to the common person and peasant in particular has been described as one of the first missions of Swedish popular adult education. In 1833 another interesting institution was created, inspired by a British example. It was the Swedish Society for the Dissemination of Useful Knowledge, which started the wide-spread information brochure 'Läsning för folket' (Reading for the People). In 1840 and

47

1850 a new adult education event took place, viz. 'bildungs'-circles and workers associations, which can be seen more as a form of group lectures than as a precursor of the Swedish concept of a study circle. More than 100 years ago, at the beginning of the 1860s the first folk high schools were set up. One or two decades later, the extramural tradition of higher education started its mission. In this broad context we also have to mention the Workers' Institute with the purpose of providing broader scientific knowledge for the people.

The first Swedish independent educational association was set up in 1912, when ABF, the Workers Educational Association was created. Its main didactic methods were an effective use of the workers' library by lectures, self studies and also the study circle, which nowadays has become the most common form of adult studies in Sweden. Whereas popular adult education has a long tradition, municipal adult education and the programme for labour market training are mainly post-war products. The same goes for different examples of educational broadcasting.

Thus, adult participation in higher education has to be related to educational participation in general. Table 6:1 (page 49) shows recent Swedish statistics in this field:[3]

The total educational activity of the adult population in 1980 was 38.5%. Thus, two out of five citizens participated in some form of organized educational activity. Only 2.6% of the total population were involved in higher studies, while more than six times as many people had joined study circles.

Four forms of adult education can be mentioned in this context, i.e. folk high schools, study associations, municipal adult education and labour market training. The objectives of Swedish adult education emphasize four aspects:

• bridging the gaps in education between youths and adults
• increasing adults' ability to get involved in and to influence the development of society
• training and retraining of adults for various professional tasks, making them able to influence direction and changes of working conditions, thereby also contributing to full employment and progress in society
• fulfilling adults' individual wishes for education and giving them opportunities to supplement their youth education.

People with short education (six or seven years at school) are the groups with high priority in today's adult education. There are, however, considerable difficulties in filling classes and study groups with students from this category and because of that there are comparatively good opportuni-

**Table 6:1** Educational participation in Sweden by course and organizer and age, 1980
**Source** *SCB (1983)*

| Organizer | 16-24 | 25-44 | 45-64 | 65-74 | Sum |
|---|---|---|---|---|---|
| Study association | 141 | 201 | 158 | 119 | 166 |
| Correspondence inst. | 2 | 3 | 2 | 1 | 2 |
| Employers | 49 | 132 | 93 | 2 | 89 |
| Trade unions | 25 | 44 | 30 | 2 | 89 |
| Labour market board | 22 | 22 | 10 | 4 | 16 |
| Radio & TV | - | 1 | 1 | - | 1 |
| Folk high school | 4 | 3 | - | 1 | 2 |
| Mun. adult education | 19 | 33 | 10 | 6 | 20 |
| State adult educ. | 2 | 3 | 1 | - | 2 |
| Compulsory school | 131 | 1 | - | - | 22 |
| Upper sec. school | 181 | 6 | 1 | - | 33 |
| Higher education | 44 | 40 | 8 | 4 | 26 |
| Other | 94 | 63 | 35 | 26 | 55 |
| Total activity | 575 | 448 | 304 | 155 | 385 |
| Non-students | 425 | 552 | 696 | 845 | 615 |
| Total sum | 1000 | 1000 | 1000 | 1000 | 1000 |

ties for young people to take part in various forms of adult education.[4]

## Folk high schools and study circles

There are more than 120 folk high schools providing general civic education. One half of the schools are run by voluntary organizations and the other half by county councils. The schools have great freedom to decide on content of education and form of tuition. Studies at folk high schools may give qualifications required for admission to higher education and upper secondary education (table 6:2, page 50).

**Table 6:2**  Participation level in different courses at folk high schools
Source  *NBE, LB 83* part II

| Fiscal | Number of students | |
|---|---|---|
| year | Winter course | Shorter courses |
| **1948/49** | 6 300 | 1800 |
| 1958/59 | 9 000 | 5 000 |

| | ▷ 30 weeks | 15 – 30 weeks | ◁ 15 weeks |
|---|---|---|---|
| 1968/69 | 12000 | 1 500 | 11 800 |
| 1973/74 | 13 400 | 2 200 | 44 000 |
| 1978/79 | 12 400 | 3 000 | 197 700 |
| 1979/80 | 12 700 | 3 300 | 220 000 |
| 1980/81 | 13 300 | 3 700 | 249 000 |

The table shows a dynamic change in provision of courses during the seventies. The number of short courses organized together with trade unions and other interest groups increased tremendously during this period.

Ten national adult educational associations administer education in study circles. The associations are linked to voluntary organizations such as trade unions, interest groups, political parties etc and have great liberty in choosing the content of the studies. Participation in study circles is usually a spare time activity. The content of popular education covers a wide range of subjects such as societal issues, humanistic perspectives, trade union matters, religious subjects, languages, handicrafts. The provision of courses and subjects reflect policies and ideologies in the respective popular movement. Study circles are the most common form of Swedish adult education. It has to be mentioned, however, that the table below does not reflect individual participants. A number of study circle participants may appear in more than one study circle (table 6:3, page 51).

The drastic change in level of participation in study circles can partly be explained by a new state regulation and a new system of resource allocation. Prior to a reform of 1981/82, the independent study associations received state financial support in relation to the number of participants. The new regulation sets an upper limit to how many study circles can be provided by

**Table 6:3**  Participation level in study circles between 1979 and 1981
Source  *(NBE) LB 83* part II

| Fiscal year | Number of study circles | Number of participants | Number of 'study hours' |
|---|---|---|---|
| 1979/80 | 334 881 | 3 036 434 | 10 781 819 |
| 1980/81 | 309 762 | 2 829 008 | 10 241 355 |
| 1981/82 | 264 504 | 2 307 691 | 8 076 653 |

a certain study association. If the number of participants extends beyond the upper limit, the study associations will receive greatly reduced support for the so called 'extra students'.

The system bears some similarity to the method of resource allocation in higher education, and one of the main motives behind it is to control public expenditures in the field of adult education. Another policy argument was to give the study associations increasing autonomy in deciding how to use their financial resources. Thus, the new regulation eliminated extensive sub-regulation and bureaucratic control from the state.[5]

## The development of municipal adult education

Municipal adult education (komvux) corresponds to the higher level of nine-year compulsory school and to upper secondary school. Municipal adult education is financed mainly through government grants.

National schools of distance adult education supplement municipal adult education and provide courses leading to the same kind of officially recognized qualifications. They are primarily intended for people who are unable to take part in 'komvux'. Studies involve a combination of correspondence courses and teacher-directed courses – usually in periods of five weeks – or else correspondence studies only.

Basic adult education (grundvux) and educational training are also provided by municipal adult schools. Basic education aims at enabling adults, immigrants and natives, to master a level of reading, writing and elementary mathematics equivalent to the sixth year of the nine-year compulsory school.

Vocational training programmes are geared to meeting individual needs in underprivileged groups as well as regional needs. Specific vocational training has no equivalent in upper secondary education and consists of shorter training programmes aiming at improved professional competence but without officially recognized certificates.

51

The system of municipal adult education was created on July 1, 1968 with the purpose of providing competence based adult education on secondary and upper secondary school levels. In the early seventies, the government recommended that the Swedish Riksdag give municipal adult education a more compensatory profile and an active role in bridging the educational gaps in society.[6] The extent of municipal adult education is presented in table 6:4 below:

Table 6:4 Different forms of formal adult education, i.e. municipal adult education, basic adult education, and state schools of adult education (the last form comprises only distance education). Source   NBE; internal statistics

| | Municipal adult education | | | | Basic adult ed | State schools |
|---|---|---|---|---|---|---|
| | Grade 7-9 | Upper second. | Voca-tional | Total | | |
| 77/78 | 97 200 | 119 500 | 58 300 | 275 000 | 2 700 | 19 400 |
| 79/80 | 109 700 | 151 200 | 60 100[1] | 321 000[1] | 5 600 | 20 600 |
| 81/82 | 91 900 | 161 100 | 65 000[1] | 318 000[1] | 10 200 | 18 800 |

1 Additional enrolments in vocational courses for unemployed people:
   1979/80   8 700
   1981/82   7 700

The objective of providing basic adult education was a main task for municipal adult education during the seventies. This goal-orientation is also crucial during the eighties, when the system is faced with an interesting transition. Firstly, there are increasing signs that basic adult education really is provided for underprivileged and socially handicapped groups. Secondly, increasing attention is being paid at policy level to vocational courses and programmes within municipal adult education. Thirdly, the Swedish Riksdag has taken a decision on the adult education curriculum in this field.

The arguments behind the new reform (l-vux 82) have an andragogic background. Prior to this reform, municipal adult education had the same syllabus and curricula as traditional secondary and upper-secondary schools. Now and onwards municipal adult education is supposed to give the same quality as the other school forms, but with another curriculum and not identical content. The general curriculum idea is the division of programmes and courses into modules in a serial and hierarchical system.

The first module is similar to basic adult education at secondary school level. The second, third and fourth modules represent different phases at upper secondary school level. Each subject is divided into more basic aspects and areas of more advanced study. The general educational idea can be summarized by this quotation the new adult education curriculum:[7]

> Mature students do not have the same starting point as young persons. Many of them study subjects relating to their occupations or to a closely defined objective. This should influence the selection of subject matter. It is inappropriate for all adults to take the same courses as young persons, and it is unnecessary for all adult students to read all parts of a course to the same extent as young persons. To facilitate adjustment to the needs and interests of the participants, all courses are divided up into a basic and advanced section.
>
> The basic section usually covers all the subject matter which the participants require in order to go on to the next course (stage). In the advanced section, the participants choose different assignments according to their individual needs and interests. In other words, they give priority to one part of the course at the expense of other parts. The participants should also be enabled to choose their working methods for the advanced section. Studies can, for example, be organized in the form of projects or problem areas. The advanced section should be spread out over the duration of the course and only part of it should occur at the end of the course.
>
> In certain subjects, students taking the advanced section of the course have to choose certain items which are not in themselves necessary to the course (stage) they are taking but are necessary foundation if they are planning to continue their studies of the subject.

The idea of an adult education curriculum is both interesting and challenging. It has at least two kinds of consequences in the field of adult higher education. Apart from the difficulties of implementing a new educational regulation (with all its problems for counsellors and adult students) it is interesting to analyse the long-term impact on recruitment to and study patterns in higher education. Secondly, it would be interesting to discuss questions of higher education curriculum in this context. What would be the educational impact of giving adult students in higher education 'the same qualities' as young students, but not 'identical contents'? And is this idea possible to realize in an integrated system of higher education? These questions are vital in a new effort to test subject knowledge of students in municipal adult education. At the secondary and upper-secondary level we have two parallel systems, but we have only one unitary system of higher education.

## Labour market training and staff development programmes

The two parts of adult education bearing the least pronounced relation to higher education are labour market training and in-plant personnel training. Labour market training is administered by government authorities. The purpose of labour market training is to provide vocational training for persons who are unemployed or in danger of unemployment. At labour market training centres there are also programmes for preparatory education and training for professions with labour shortages. Studying at a labour market centre is a full-time occupation.

**Table 6:5**   Participation level in labour market training
Source   *NBE*, **internal statistics**

*Labour market training*

|  | AMU-C | Ind. | Ord. syst | Other | Total |
|---|---|---|---|---|---|
| 77/78 | 61 000 | 61 000 | 26 000 | 7 000 | 155 000 |
| 79/80 | 78 000 | 7 000 | 32 000 | 3 000 | 120 000 |
| 81/82 | 69 000 | 15 000 | 18 000 | 2 000 | 104 000 |

Personnel training and personnel development in employment are of course very important parts of adult education and recurrent education. Goals, contents and forms vary considerably, however, from one organization or field to another. Participation in internal training and development at work can often yield experience which is useful in higher education. One of the main reasons for giving credit to job experience in connection with higher education admission was in fact that in many cases it conferred competence for further studies. Table 6 (page 55) shows the number of participants in trade union and other non-formal adult education (excluding folk high schools and study circles):

It is difficult to get accurate statistics of participation level in non-formal adult education. The report of the government commission on labour market training and in-service training presents some figures.[8] (table 6:7, page 56)

It is obvious that the participation level is highly correlated with prior education. Employees with higher education have at least twice as many

**Table 6:6**  Participation level in non-formal adult education within trade unions and other organizations.
Source  *NBE, LB-83* Part II

| Trade unions | Participants | | |
|---|---|---|---|
| | 1979/80 | 1980/81 | 1981/82 |
| LO | 14 641 | 15 850 | 14 907 |
| TCO | 6 509 | 6 490 | 5 683 |
| SACO/SR | 1 497 | 1 418 | 1 545 |
| SALF | - | 436 | 231 |
| SAC | 151 | 258 | 216 |
| | 22 798 | 24 452 | 22 582 |
| *Other organiza-tions* | | | |
| LRF | 914 | 961 | 951 |
| SHIO | 66 | 137 | 137 |
| SRF | - | 17 | 32 |
| | 980 | 1 115 | 1 120 |
| Total sum | 23 778 | 25 567 | 23 702 |

opportunities as employees with no post-compulsory education. Thus, educational background tend to be a more important decision than age determinant.[8]

## The evaluation of adult education reforms – some concluding remarks

A systems perspective of the kind presented above is, of course, highly schematic and generalized, but it should be a serviceable point of departure for the formulation of some general questions concerning the role of higher education in adult and recurrent education. Historically speaking, for example, it is interesting to elucidate the way in which the traditions and ideological backgrounds of the various forms of education have developed and changed. In the new vocational system of higher education in Sweden,

**Table 6:7** Proportion of employees who participated in adult education during working hours in the last 12 months.
Source  *SOU 1983:22* page 176

| Educational level | 1975 | | | 1979 | | |
|---|---|---|---|---|---|---|
| | Men | Women | Total | Men | Women | Total |
| Secondary school | 17.9 | 12.6 | 15.5 | 23.7 | 20.1 | 21.9 |
| Upper secondary school | 34.1 | 24.0 | 29.8 | 44.6 | 34.3 | 39.8 |
| Higher education | 54.6 | 48.9 | 52.1 | 59.1 | 52.3 | 55.9 |
| Total | 30.4 | 22.7 | 27.0 | 39.1 | 31.9 | 35.9 |

the step from general education to vocational preparation or from *Bildung* to *Ausbildung* has been further accentuated. This, however, is not to say that the universities have always been concerned with Bildung and the refinement of intellect. The first universities in the 13th century were primarily training establishments for officials, priests and other groups, while during other periods universities were more exclusively concerned with Bildung[9]

From the point of view of principle the technological challenge and the vocational 'boom' can be met in at least two different ways. Firstly, we could do our best to try to identify the needs and demands of professional up-grading and the development of a better technical or instrumental knowledge. Secondly, we could underline the need for value-clarification approaches and other efforts that increase our capacity to understand technology in the context of human beings surrounded by ideas and traditions. We see no definite choice between a *competence-approach* and a *bildung or understanding approach*, rather the need for a functional balance, organizational differentiation and diversity of curricula in the relations between higher education and adult education.

The relation between higher education and different forms of adult education is a crucial but difficult policy problem in Sweden. The technological challenge and the need for a modernized citizen knowledge and professional competence call for a closer collaboration between higher education, municipal adult education, labour market training, and also new programmes and courses within the field of upper secondary schooling. Thus, there is a continuous need for renewal of curricula and programmes in fields as technology and computerization, social and administrative systems, teaching and learning and the development of new production techniques. To a large extent, this challenge has to be met at regional and local levels, where a new network of contacts between educational authorities, labour market representatives and trade unions is needed.[10]

The future discussion of the issues raised in this chapter will probably be stimulated by a recently published report of a governmental task-force on the outcome of the Swedish adult education reforms of the seventies.[11] The report could be summarized as follows:

• the reform of adult education has broadened the provision and volume of programmes and courses during the seventies and also increased the total level of adult participation, while the objective of stressing the need of increasing equality of opportunity has not been realized.
• furthermore, the report quotes Swedish research showing that adult education participation tends to increase the general level of cultural and political resources of the individual. Adult education also leads to stronger self-confidence and broadened societal horizons.
• finally, the report outlines a programme that is supposed to increase the participation of adults with restricted or non-existent education experiences. The priority groups are, according to the report,:
– adults with shorter compulsory education than nine years
– adults unable to read, write and count
– adults with different handicaps
– adults in unemployment
– immigrants with restricted educational background
• one central idea of this programme of affirmative action is that a certain amount of the state funds should be ear-marked for the priority groups
• another idea of the report is that in-service training and staff development programmes tend to be more and more important components in Swedish adult education. Thus, they cannot be isolated from general adult education policy.

The report also stresses the need of active recruitment measures such as out-reach activities in the work place in combination with group-recruitment. Finally, it has to be mentioned that this governmental report does not discuss the role of adults in higher education. Rather, its main focus is basic adult education in a broader social perspective.

# 7　Recurrent education, organizational flexibility and the notion of higher learning

## Objectives of recurrent education

The idea of recurrent education constitutes a turning point in Swedish educational policy.[1] Previously, education had been regarded mainly as 'youth injection' and elementary schooling as an adequate foundation for more vocational education or induction into working life. Another explanation for this more static view of education is that a trade, once mastered, would last for life. Things have now changed. Only a small percentage of compulsory school leavers go straight into employment. The working population is faced with an accelerating process of structural change, necessitating a revision of their qualifications. In addition, recurrent education is needed in order to close the gaps between different groups and also for economic reasons, i.e. as a means of distributing educational opportunities more appropriately throughout the individual life cycle.[1] From the viewpoint of the individual, recurrent education means:

- increased opportunities of alternating between education, gainful employment and other activities
- opportunities of rectifying mistaken choices and, in the course of one's life, changing specialities, jobs, life-style, etc.
- opportunities of achieving closer links between one's own, accumulated knowledge and experience and various types of education

- greater awareness in terms of educational motivation and the formulation of educational needs.

From the viewpoint of the educational system, recurrent education demands:

- the elimination of dead ends and inflexible study programmes
- a generous selection of extension courses and opportunities for supplementary study
- a more flexible system of courses, with longer and more continuous study programmes divided into modules, phases or individualized programmes
- closer regional and local co-operation between different educational mandators.

## Upper secondary schools and recurrent education

Recurrent education is mainly an organizational strategy aiming at a more flexible and open network of educational routes through the life span of all citizens. In this context it is very interesting to analyze the way in which different qualitative goals of education can be asserted in a system of recurrent education. Examples of such goals are deep-level understanding vs surface knowledge, the balance between vocational knowledge and general education, the links between science, culture and society and the question of where and when specialization should be developed. These issues are of great importance in the current Swedish policy debate, which is reflected by the central position which recurrent education occupies in the Government Upper Secondary Schools Bill.[2]

> Upper secondary schooling ought in my opinion to be one of the natural foundation stones of an educational system based on the principle of recurrent education. This being so, upper secondary schools must, first of all, be built up so as to prepare everybody for both vocational activity and further education. Secondly, supplementary education must be made available as a sequel to two or three years' upper secondary schooling, either immediately after completion of a line of upper secondary schools or following a period of economic activity.

The emphasis on recurrent education is also an essential element of the policy of the Swedish National Board of Education. The previously published long-term assessment (LB 84) devotes considerable attention to recurrent education as an underlying principle of the further reform of post-compulsory education, not least in view of the reform of upper secondary schooling.[3]

When it was first launched at the end of the 1960s, the idea of recurrent education prompted an interesting discussion concerning the interaction of compulsory school, upper secondary school, adult education and higher education. The most ambitious interpretation of the concept demanded a thorough transformation of the entire educational system with a view to facilitating   alternation between education and employment throughout the individual life cycle. Another interpretation was that recurrent education above all implied the use of compensatory adult education to bridge the educational gaps between different generations and social classes. A more pragmatic view of recurrent education has stressed the importance of further and subsequent education for those who are already economically active or, purely and simply, the idea of various forms of alternation between education and employment.

The idea of a constructive link between upper secondary schooling, higher education and other forms of adult education constitutes an important point of departure for the further development of post-compulsory education. Adult education must be allowed to develop on its own terms instead of becoming a residual product of reforms of compulsory schooling.[4]

This makes it important to stress the links between upper secondary schooling and parts of adult education and not to allow the development of adult education to be governed by the conditions to which youth education is subject. The NBE therefore wishes to safeguard a richly diverisfied network of adult education bases on a variety of fundamental ideas, with variegated amenities and a diversity of educational methods. For adult adjustment is not just a matter of different educational motives and other aspects of the socio-educational environment, frequently including pronounced social and geographical commitments. Adult adjustment is also a question of developing the content and routines of education in such a way that it will genuinely follow on from previous experience and competence and provide opportunities of utilising practical and vocational experience in the teaching context. Adult adjustment therefore demands a more differentiated system of courses and, in many cases, individualised study programmes.

## Experience of higher education

The concept of recurrent education was also a vital ingredient in the thinking of the U 68 Commission and is also enshrined in the Higher Education Act. The idea of recurrent education is not confined to higher studies but applies to the whole of post-compulsory education. In addition, it is directly related to personnel education and the conditions governing learning at work. The instruments of recurrent education within the higher education system are the rules of admission, with their emphasis on work experience, the idea of dividing long study programmes into phases and the development of short-cycle courses providing opportunities of subsequent and further education for the economically active. Fundamentally, recurrent education was a strategy of organizational reform, aimed at transforming the entire formal education system in such a way as to facilitate alternation between education, employment and other activities.

How is the idea of recurrent education viewed today? First of all we may note that the concept has once again come into the focus of educational policy, following a certain decline during the closing years of the 1970s. It is not outmoded, even though it has come in for criticism. Where higher education is concerned, the idea of developing intermediate qualifications or intermediate admissions in prolonged study programmes has met with fierce resistance. Quite clearly, the designation of work experience as an additional qualification for young students has led to an alternation between education and employment which would definitely not have materialised otherwise – at least, not to the same extent. The provision of short-cycle courses too has evoked a powerful response from employed persons with an interest in subsequent or further education. And by international standards, the Swedish higher education system is well to the fore where adult participation is concerned.

The reform of upper secondary and the new curriculum for municipal adult education should make opportunities of recurrent education more extensive than they were at the beginning of the seventies. Growing opportunities of regional planning, course development and co-operation between higher education, upper secondary schooling and municipal adult education are a contributory factor here. Labour market training and folk high schools are essential interlocutors in a system of recurrent education, as are various forms of in-house training. The intermediate admissions and qualifications of municipal adult education and the interaction between basic and advanced studies in this context are also in keeping with the idea of recurrent education, which is very much a question of the individual being able, successively and by stages, to augment his education as a means of updating outmoded qualifications and acquiring broader civic competence.

61

## The need for a deeper analysis of educational perspectives and knowledge ideals of recurrent education

Recurrent education is primarily an organizational concept. Apart from its emphasis on work experience and vocational competence, this concept expresses a very vague view of knowledge. This calls for a closer analysis of what happens to qualitative educational goals (so called 'bildungs-ideals' or principles of high culture) when interaction between upper secondary schooling, municipal adult education, folk high schools and other adult education including higher education is developed according to the principle of recurrent education. What is the balance between general education and common learning on the one side and vocational education on the other? In this connection, special attention needs to be paid to the following problems:

• The extent to which the content, resources and organization of the new upper secondary school facilitate the development of qualitative educational objectives and meaningful educational content for different kinds of students.
• The prospects of different kinds of work-study programmes for school-leavers without substantial basic education
• The possibilities of promoting deeper subject understanding in modular courses in upper secondary schools, in the adult curriculum in municipal adult education or higher education programmes on courses.
• The possibilities of developing constructive links between different kinds of work experience, practical training and subject content, both in upper secondary school and in higher education.

Inevitably, the organizational transformation of Swedish post-compulsory education calls for a deeper analysis of curriculum ideas, changing subject content and current definitions of knowledge.

Long-term policy development and research as well as local development and research activities concerning successive changes to post-compulsory education will therefore have to pay special attention to these problems. And this is particulary pertinent to the egalitarian aspirations which have been typical of Swedish educational policy as a whole and which also apply to the reform of upper secondary schooling in particular.[5]

> The role of upper secondary schools as the foundation of lifelong learning also makes added demands on the internal working environ-ment. School work must be conducted in such a way as to give all young persons a positive attitude towards learning. There must be better utilisation and development of the inherent desire of all young

persons for knowledge and competence. During their upper secondary schooling, therefore, students must also be given an opportunity of building up the self-esteem and self-confidence which can result from the achievement of educational goals which they themselves have helped to define.

## Impediments to recurrent education

Although there are certain indications of opportunities of recurrent education being better today than they were at the beginning of the 1970s, great impediments still remain. Two of them will be mentioned here. Firstly, one should emphasize that the idea of recurrent education cannot be realised solely within the framework of the education system. From the very beginning, changes in working life, the creations of a new work organization, the introduction of new methods of production and the resultant demands for qualifications were emphasized as the foundation of recurrent education. Secondly, it is important to make clear that a viable system of educational leave and educational finance for adults constitutes an essential prerequisite for realising the idea of recurrent education. Statutory entitlement to educational leave has existed in Sweden since 1975. This entitlement does not confer any rights to educational finance, which has to be separately applied for.

We know today that neither loan-grant assistance nor special adult study assistance is properly adapted to the private economic circumstances of students. In addition, many economically active adults hesitate to burden their future economy with recurrent amortization payments, which in turn leads them to study part-time and carry on working. Many students of all ages hardly have time to penetrate different fields of knowledge in such a way as to satisfy educational ideals of a more qualitative nature. Theoretically speaking, there is no discrepancy between recurrent education and a more qualitative view of education. In the actual educational situation, and, with the resources currently available, however, the idea of recurrent education is liable to be watered down and the result may sometimes be a hastily acquired superficial understanding of certain specialized fields.

The results of the follow-up of the new organization of studies in higher education, and especially of short-cycle courses in the humanities and social sciences, provide a further indication of this risk. Swedish studies into these issues have shown that students have the same general educational motives as before the reform of higher education. The one vital difference is that today, due partly to the organization of short-cycle courses, studies tend to be more a question of acreage than depth. From a qualitative point of view, any Open Door policy, must, in the long run, broaden the adult students' knowledge perspectives and horizons. Otherwise it is not an Open Door in a more genuine academic sense.

The development of the new upper secondary school has an essential bearing on the content, organization and future of adult education. The interaction of upper secondary school, higher education, adult education and popular education can be viewed both in the short and the long term. Various experimental themes are outlined in the development-programme that is now being planned at regional and local levels as mandated by the Government and Riksdag. As regards the connection between upper secondary school and adult education, collaboration has been proposed between upper secondary schools and municipal adult education in sparsely populated rural areas, as well as experimental vocational education, pooling of facilities and co-ordinated planning involving upper secondary schools, municipal adult education and labour market training. Most immediately, this is a matter of pooling resources and exploiting them more efficiently, for example by tailoring educational amenities more closely to regional demand.

## Recurrent education and new school reforms – some conclusions

Looking further ahead and bearing in mind the ideas of recurrent education implicit in the reform of upper secondary schooling, there are of course many other questions which present themselves. What demands does upper secondary school have to meet if it is really to constitute the first step in a process of recurrent education? How will the proposed vocational and credential extension courses actually work out in the future? How will supplementary studies in the form of municipal adult education affect the future of higher education? And last but not least, how will the distribution of education in society tomorrow be influenced by the fact of upper secondary schooling (municipal follow-up responsibilities included) being 'substantially, although not formally, compulsory'.[6]

Is there any risk of eleven years' schooling for all young persons widening the educational gap between them and the still sizeable contingents of the adult population who have neither attended the nine-year compulsory school nor acquired any further educational experience at upper secondary level? And how will the various generations learn to understand and apply new technology in the community and at work? The answers to these questions are neither given nor predestined. They will to a very great extent depend on the ability of governments, politicians and the organizers of adult education to support and develop both credential adult education and popular education.

Further development of the idea of recurrent education will demand more penetrating curricular analysis, including a closer scrutiny of the preconditions governing the interaction of work experience, vocational knowledge and subject knowledge. In this connection, special attention should be paid to different methods of individually or collectively crediting previous education and experience. The essential premise of the recurrent education model at post-secondary level is the existence of a system of programmes which are to be shaped more flexibly by means of a judicious balance between basic and advanced studies, opportunities of intermediate qualification and admissions to individual courses forming part of a programme. The degrees of liberty within this model are, to a large extent, determined by the planning models and ideals of study organization espoused by the educational mandators, not by the needs and circumstances of the individual. The North American ideas concerning recognition of prior experience represent an attempt in this latter direction; the RPE model starts with the overall competence and experiential background of the individual, to which it then proceeds to add the necessary courses and sub-items.

We also need to refine premises of educational planning and curricular theory with a view to a more flexible, adaptable programme structure. In context of this kind, there will always be a place for the idea of alternation between theory and practice or between education and employment. And so the idea of recurrent education is still with us, although less grandiloquent and less inflated than it was in the seventies. Even if the educational system has not been successfully organized in keeping with this principle, there is no mistaking the convergence between the educational patterns of young persons and mature students and the idea of recurrent education.[7]

# 8     Linking adult and higher education to working life – policy problems in Swedish post-compulsory education

## Adult higher education and the technological challenge

The reform of 1977 created an organizational framework for the interplay between higher education and working life. U 68 did not treat questions of subject matter content and higher education curricula. It is apparent, however, that the reform had a fundamental impact on knowledge content and programme construction. Firstly, the reform implementation stimulated curriculum development in various educational sectors and especially in the sector of economic, administrative and social professions and the medical and paramedical sector. Secondly, the incorporation of prior non-academic knowledge traditions into the unitary system of higher education contributed to new ways of defining the concept of higher learning.

The general policy, however, has not been to 'academize' vocational programmes, but to broaden the theoretical programmes and to give vocational programmes better links to research. Thirdly, it is interesting to analyze to what extent 'adultification' influences curriculum content and knowledge definitions in higher education. The new Higher Education Act stresses the importance of recognizing and using the students' life and work experiences. We begin to get a comprehensive picture of the pattern of experiential sharing in different programmes and courses. We know less, however, about the possible long-term impact of knowledge definitions in Swedish higher education.[1]

Like most Western countries Sweden is faced with a rapid technological | *10*
transition and structural changes in working life. The computerization of
production techniques and public services contributes to a new industrial,
social and cultural environment. Inflation is today not only related to
currency, but also to human capital. Professional competence rooted in old
production techniques can lose its value over a night. Some researchers
argue that the new production technologies will lead to a degradation of
human beings and their competence, while others perceive the current
transition as a challenge and development. Independent of educational
perspective, it is not easy to define the future role of adult higher education
or adult education in general. It is also difficult to make value-neutral
descriptions of expected qualifications in different job-situations.

Let us take a Swedish study on professional knowledge and training in
industry as an example.[2] Three kinds of work are discussed:

*1* Routine work
*2* Work that requires knowledge acquired primarily in working life
*3* Work that demands formal education

Two central questions in the study are; a) what kind of qualification is
needed for different jobs, b) what period of in-service training and work
adjustment is necessary in order to cope with expectations.

According to the definitions in the study, routine work has no significant
expectations of prior education and job-experience. In general, however,
employers prefer persons with educational backgrounds which would
enable to be used for other tasks further on. The main recruitment criteria
tend to be personality-aspects such as positive work attitudes, loyalty, good
health etc. Jobs with expectations of professional development and training
within the work place underscore specific qualifications related to production technology and patterns of work supervision of certain enterprises,
factories or firms. The third category, jobs demanding formal education, are
mainly white collar work at a professional level, but can also include skilled
workers with long prior professional training. The expected qualifications
are not production-specific, but general and well-defined. The most
common method is external recruitment as there are limited possibilities of
up-grading skilled workers or other employees.

Official statistics provide a general picture of the qualification levels of
white-collar workers and blue-collar workers in the Swedish industry.[3] The
figures for white-collar workers are: (table 8:1, page 68)

Unfortunately, there are no similar categories for blue-collar workers, but
the following figures provide some aspects of training opportunities: (table
8:2, page 68)

Table 8:1

| Leading position | Independent work | Qualified work | Routine work |
|---|---|---|---|
| 8% | 51% | 28% | 15% |

Table 8:2

| Skilled workers | Qualified tempo-work | Less qualified tempo-work |
|---|---|---|
| 34% | 52% | 14% |

These figures have to be interpreted with care, as they comprise only a minor part of the Swedish labour market (208 000 + 152 000). They give, however, a general background of the relation between educational opportunities and job qualifications.

It is important to clarify to what extent this qualification structure is accurate or obsolete in relation to the new production technology developed in working life and in the public service sector. Another recently published Swedish study analyzes the impact of the 'new technology' on productivity, employment and working hours.[4] The concept of new technology contains various aspects of micro-electronic applications as computers, robots, and new information service systems.

There are, according to the report, different opinions in the international debate whether the new technology will lead to mass unemployment or not. There is, however, increasingly shared knowledge that the technological impact can show strong differences between various sectors. Thus, micro-electronics will increase employment and create new professional groups in some sectors, and at the same time diminish or eliminate production methods and occupational categories in other sectors.

The technological challenge raises the need for an educational challenge. It is quite evident that the latter challenge cannot only be met within formal institutions of adult or higher education. A main part of the professional development and up-grading of skill and knowledge must take place within industry or the public service system. It is, however, also obvious, that formal adult education including higher education will have a growing importance in the future.

The rapid change of the knowledge and competence-structure calls for 'new platforms of knowledge and experience' of working people. Thus, we need both broader societal and civic knowledge and more specialized and high-technology oriented knowledge. Otherwise, there is an increasing risk that we will get overeducated employees and undereducated citizens. An educational programme cannot only adapt adults to a rapid and seemingly uncontrolled technological development. The educational mission must also be to give workers and citizens cognitive and intellectual tools to understand and influence this development.

Another important contribution to the Swedish debate and policy analysis has been a government task force on education and productivity.[5] In the final report, the task force stresses the need for more active and dynamic educational planning in order to meet national and regional needs. Education is viewed as a tool of knowledge investment for the future. Thus, the task force recommends the government to educate and train more people in certain sectors than is demanded presently or anticipated in the future. Knowledge fields such as biotechnological systems and new materials are examples of such development areas.

Further, the task force underscores the need to stimulate activities of in-schooling and competence-adaptation in different sectors of working life. The formal educational system provides a broader knowledge platform and the development of certain professional skills. To this platform must be added specific information, skills and experiences. Finally, the task force of education and productivity focusses on higher education and municipal adult education as agents for commissioned adult education. The idea is that employers can 'buy knowledge and competence' from the systems of adult and higher education.

## Liberal education in a vocational context?

Undoubtedly, there has been a strong trend of vocationalism in current policy perspectives of adult and higher education. The task force on education and productivity has also discussed the need for special courses or programmes linking upper secondary education or higher education to different areas of working life. These courses are intended to function as bridges between formal schooling and the work environment and qualification structure in different work situations. There are evident similarities between these courses and the North-American concept of cooperative education. The policy towards vocationalism is also expressed through a growing interest in practical exercises, college sponsored work experience and field work. The student's set of experiences comprises both prior life and work experiences and experiential dimensions of the curriculum.

The tension between the broad educational ideals such as those of liberal education, humanities and common learning   on the one hand and the increased demand for vocational training and skill up-grading on the other is significant in current policy debate today in western countries.[6] Ideas of liberal education are embedded in a labour market context. The economic crisis and the technological challenge put heavy claims on skill up-grading and more specialized study programmes for various professions. State support granted to public institutions of adult higher education is very much influenced by this tendency towards vocationalism, as are also the employers' increasing influence upon further education and continued training of their employees.

If we take the USA as an example, adult students in higher education are getting more and more dependent on a system of study finance governed by the companies, and the study programmes to be chosen are also a question for the employer to decide upon. It is evident that it is still difficult for liberal education to compete in a hardening economic climate, but there is still some hope. Thus, many people maintain that broader study programmes would be the best solution when facing the claims for specialized knowledge (not least within the technical sector). The programme for Science, Technology and Society (STS), as well as existing departments for social science with their own research activities – both at M.I.T. – are very interesting in this connection.[7] The interplay between liberal education and the vocational boom is not so easy to describe in simple terminology. In Sweden, there is, as in many other western countries a debate on the links between education and culture. Should all institutions of post-compulsory education share a common core of culture and liberal education? We have study programmes in the field of culture and humanities, but not the notion of liberal colleges, if we exclude the swedish folk high school.

From the point of view of curriculum theory it is interesting to compare patterns of thinking and problem solving of liberal art subjects and a vocational or technical subject e.g. auto-mechanics. What were the pedagogical conditions for the various subject contents of technically oriented subjects and those aiming at insight and understanding respectively? What was actually the core of higher education? If liberal education comprises higher intellectual skill, methods of advancing knowledge in a field, and transmitting a common body of knowledge, what is the specific core of a vocational subject? Is the concept of a 'vocational subject' really a useful tool? Current Swedish policy debate questions the idea that vocational knowledge has to be 'uncritical', narrow and specialized. Rather, it argues that vocational subjects have their own forms of critical thinking.

It is not only on theoretical grounds that there are many arguments for the usefulness of liberal education/broader frames of references in a specialized and profession-oriented way of thinking. Good professional knowledge is not strictly specialized technical knowledge, or the knowledge of facts, but the ability to think in a parallel way on different levels of complexity, to combine intuition and analysis, to relate the technical optimum to various moral/ethical predicaments, and to experience a dynamic interplay between scientific knowledge and everyday experiences. Educational planning is facing various paradoxes and contradictions. To meet the claims for more specialized knowledge we also have to provide broader frames of reference and general knowledge ('fringe knowledge'). A constructive tension is necessary between the educational frames of reference and the requirements of working life.

## Do Part-time Students have Part-time Identities?

The main purpose of this book has been to give a broad image of the phenomenon of 'adultification' of Swedish higher education.[8] One consequence of this development is that we can no longer talk about *the* young student. Instead, the student population comprises a variety of young and adult students with different educational backgrounds, social roles, professional obligations and motives of study. Thus, one cannot plan for young students or for adults, but for more heterogenous student groups. From an educational point of view, the new situation can be seen as both a challenge and a risk. The challenge lies in the fact that many adult students have a considerable amount of life and work experiences, which could be utilised more in the teaching and learning process. On the other hand, an increasing use of experiential learning tends to be perceived as a threat to traditional academic knowledge. Thus, many adult students tend to have a more pragmatic knowledge view supported by an experienced need for practical utilisation, while we university teachers are more inclined to care for the specific subject values and knowledge traditions. In this context, 'adultification' also leads to a growing confrontation between different knowledge ideals and traditions. The meetings of traditions and perspectives are very dynamic, experiential, and also challenging to traditional ideals. Thus, it is more and more important to clarify in what directions 'adultification' influences knowledge traditions and concept development in Swedish higher education.

Another consequence of 'adultification' lies in what we have called

71

patterns of student life. Today, Swedish students in higher education have a number of obligations parallel to their studies. Both young and adult students combine higher studies and work. Others have to find their learning strategies in a context of social restrictions and contradictory obligations, i.e. a limited time budget caused by family, work and other activities. Thus, many of these students have a part-time identity as a student. They are not isolated from society, but, rather, an integrated part of it. It would be interesting to compare the socialisation effects of students with a part-time identity and students with a full-time identity. When Oscar Olsson made his statement almost 60 years ago it was easy to see who was a student at university level. Today, with increasing enrolment and new study patterns, it is more difficult to recognize the differences between a student and an ordinary citizen.

In fact, we have also changed the concept of student. Prior to the great reform period a student (spelled 'student' also in Swedish) was a person who had matriculated from upper secondary school, and thereby met the necessary requirements for higher studies. Today, the concept of 'student' has been changed to *studerande*, which refers to 'a person who is studying'. This is, of course, a much broader concept. And this is not only a change at a semantical level, rather it reflects the transition from a more exclusive student identity to a situation in which higher studies is only one of many aspects of the individual role set. This is not to say that Sweden has lost all its traditional student activities or academic rituals during the reform period. The social cultures of the academy have survived, not only at traditional universities such as Uppsala (founded in 1477) and Lund (1668), but also at newer universities like Stockholm, Göteborg and Umeå. It is not too challenging a hypothesis to conclude, however, that the percentage of students (or *studerande*) taking part in these activities is decreasing. Thus, the new student tends to be more of a citizen than a student, and he/she has also less time to take part in the 'student life traditions' and the hidden curriculum of our centres for higher learning.

At the same time, there are a number of signs indicating that the adult majority together with the increasing number of working students change the teaching and learning context, e.g. more group work and project studies and less traditional academic methods like lectures and self-study. Another change concerns the decreasing number of textbooks in foreign languages. There are few books in English, which nowadays tends to be accepted as a second language both for young and adult students, not to mention German or French, let alone Greek or Latin. Thus, the adult majority indirectly contributes to a more domestic or provincial knowledge setting, where work experience and occupational expectations are more important than the academic traditions, the "great classics" or foreign theoretical approaches. Further, working students and studying workers also put a strong demand on part-time studies and evening classes, which is not always an expectation shared by faculty or teachers' trade unions.

The adult majority has also been subject to a long and lasting political debate between progressive and conservative interests in Swedish society. The 'progressivists' (the social democratic party and the big trade unions of white and blue-collar workers) see the adult and working students as resources and a target group for educational equality, while the conservatives (the conservative party together with the trade union of professionals and graduates, to some extent the student unions and many traditional university professors) are in favour of young (and bright) students. In my opinion, however, the Swedish debate has been pre-occupied by recruitment and admission problems (and numbers), neglecting the need to organize the teaching and learning setting in a way which increases the retention of "risk students" and also gives more place for experiential sharing and use of the adult students as a resource in the learning process.

## The dilemma of numbers and content

The development of systems of adult higher education has to be related to the broader policy context of higher education reflected by Martin Trow's well-known distinction between elite higher education, mass higher education and universal access-higher education.[9] If we use Trow's broad categories it is possible to relate the level of participation (measured by different indices like enrolment statistics /in relation to the population in a country/, level of studies, kind and percentage of examinations) to curriculum content and educational design (that could be described on a dimension from the British notion of high culture over liberal education, vocational knowledge to more soft criteria as experiential learning or everyday experiences).

Mixing these factors together we will face the dilemma of numbers and content. An increased level of participation, by both young and adult students, necessarily leads to a redefinition of curriculum content and notions of higher learning (**Figure 8:1, page 74**).

The combinations of level of participation and curriculum content and educational design vary from country to country. Traditionally, increased participation has been solved by broadening the very concept of higher learning, and thus giving more place for vocationally oriented programmes. Thus, the expansion in American higher education has not occurred in traditional and prestigious universities, but in community colleges with

**Figure 8:1** The dilemma of numbers and content (different knowledge definition in higher education).

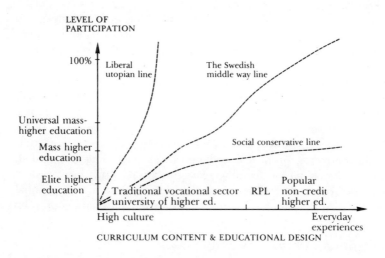

2-year and 4-year programmes. Two typical broadening measures in the U.K. have been the introduction of polytechnics and the creation of the Open University.

The Swedish way of broadening the concept of higher education has been obtained by including some of the traditionally non-academic institutions within the integrated system of higher education. The alternative routes for adults aiming at higher education study have been channelled through this system, and not by building a parallel organization for working people.

The examples mentioned above may be seen as illustrations of the fact that the level of participation has to be related to the notion of higher learning used in various countries. The British notion of 'high culture' seems to be very different from the North-American efforts of giving credits for prior experiences and experiential learning (which, of course, only represent a minor part of higher education in the U.S.A.). The Swedish concept of higher learning is a bridge built on two pillars, the scientific knowledge generated by research and theoretical study on one hand, and the knowledge and frames of references developed in working life and different professions on the other hand.

What are, from an epistemological point of view, the differences between the British notion of high culture, the ambitions to credit experiential learning and the Swedish knowledge concept with its focus on integration between research-generated knowledge and knowledge articulated in different work processes or life settings? It is not a solely theoretical matter. In practice it has obvious consequences for the ways of linking higher education knowledge to experiences and competences of adult students.

It seems to me that the level of participation in adult higher education in various countries cannot only be related to 'situational' and 'instructional' barriers to higher education, but also to the cultural and historical notions of higher learning. Starting from such an analysis it will be necessary to define the 'costs' and 'benefits' in a broad sense, of increasing the level of participation in a certain educational environment in a specific country.

What are, for example, the costs of increasing the level of participation in adult higher education by X% in a country Y? And, what is the alternative usage of these resources, and what remedial measures for already present disadvantaged adult students are involved? And to what extent can the level of participation in adult higher education be related to adult education in general? How do we define qualitative criteria of the most beneficial adult learning context on a scale from adult higher education, to adult education in general and non-formal adult education?

It is not realistic to deschool the academy and tell people to embark on their self-learning projects. On the other hand, a 100% level participation of adults in higher education programmes does not seem to be the solution the policy makers are prepared to support, especially not in times of economic stagnation and retrenchment. Further, the need for better and more adapted curricula can neither be solved with a basic core curriculum for all adult students, nor by market solutions and giving the adults what they feel they need. The challenge of future adult higher education is reflected by the tension between the broader frames of reference and critical training which forms part of higher learning and the growing need for skill-up-grading and job-related knowledge among adult students.


## Concluding remarks on conditions of policy implementation

The purpose of this report has been to present some of the general development trends and policy considerations in Swedish adult higher education. The content reflects the difficulties in obtaining more accurate statistics and also, more in-depth process-studies or case analyses. Further, most research in this field suffers from the usual disease of fragmentation. This is understandable taking into account the difficulties of developing broader and more policy-oriented research strategies. Thus, the report is more focussed towards description than analysis. Further, it is more problem-oriented than strategic or solution-oriented.

Another conclusion of this report is that we still lack sufficient knowledge and conceptual models for analyzing the impact of the reform of higher education on the level and pattern of adult participation. A further analysis has to specify reform objectives, measures taken, criteria of reform assessment and new policy issues.

The Swedish Open Door policy has to some extent contributed to the adultification of the system. The participation of adults, however, started long before the reform in the late fifties. In the early seventies, adultification fit well with the declining enrolment of young students. In the early eighties, the young students have returned thereby causing increasing competition for student places. For demographic reasons, this conflict might be articulated in the future, especially if we take the restricted financial situation into consideration.

Another policy issue is the idea of recurrent education and the adaptation of curriculum to the needs and conditions of working adults.

**Table 8:3** An outline for analyzing recurrent education as a policy issue in Swedish higher education.

| Reform objectives | Measures taken | Policy impact, criterion level | New policy issues |
|---|---|---|---|
| Recurrent education | 'New' programme structure; i.e. gen. study prog. local lines, ind. lines, separate courses, the recognition of work experience | Adults prefer sep. courses, old pattern at trad. faculties of arts sciences. Work exp. postpone/delay studies of young students. Few ind. lines. Less specified subject study. Few successful 'phased exits'. | New policy debate of the efficacy of higher education. What is relevant work experience. In search for a renewal of programme structure. Redefinition of recurrent education. |
| Increased vocationalism & a 'balanced' concept of higher learning. | A number of curricular reforms. Broadening of theoretical progr; research connections of vocational programme | All programmes in the same organization | 'La penetration scientific'. No major policy discussion on educational ideals, the quantitative frames & stud. equality in focus |

What are the realities behind the concept of recurrent education in Swedish higher education? There is not so much left of the grand ideas of recurrent education from the early seventies. The idea of reorganizing the whole formal educational system is no more a main policy orientation. On the other hand, the concept is not dead, only somewhat transformed. Two of the most successful instruments in higher education have been work experience for young students and separate courses for adults. The experiments with phased exits and educational modules have not been promising so far, if we exclude some study programmes in health and medical care organized by the county councils. On the other hand it is evident that the establishment of municipal adult education and the provision of upper secondary education for all pupils leaving the compulsory school gives a wider organizational context for recurrent education than in the mid-seventies. One of the main problems of adult higher education is to find and develop methods of connecting professional competence and skill of working adults with new knowledge and cognitive styles needed in order to cope with the technological challenge.

Apart from vocational programmes for skilled technicians and small scale programmes for nurses wanting to be doctors, there have been few curriculum experiments in the field of adult higher education. On the contrary, one can characterize the prevailing curriculum notion as a move from individualization to integration. There are few local study programmes, and even fewer individual programmes. Some shortened programmes have been changed accordingly to one integrated programme instead of two parallel programmes with various length. It is interesting to compare the integrative efforts in higher education with municipal adult education, where a new adult education curriculum has been put into practice.

Looking back on Swedish educational policy, one can question the order in which the different reform steps proceeded. There was a strong policy interest in and reform measures concerning the compulsory school system and the system of higher education. At the same time the upper secondary school system was "living a life of its own". The schools of municipal adult education was a rather newly created organization. As a consequence, the new system of higher education was promoted as an open and adult-adjusted organization, which might have stimulated many adults to take a 'direct' route to higher education without getting necessary basic knowledge through the municipal adult education. Today, when the adult education schools are established and respected in most cities, adult students may choose a more realistic study pattern.

In a comparative perspective, this phenomenon opens up a discussion of two relatively different policy perspectives. The first perspective could be labelled an *Open Door Policy* and is mainly focussed on different measures of increasing adult participation in higher education, e.g.

- A more liberal admission system recognizing real rather than formal competences of adults
- Different measures of information and counselling and introductory programmes in order to facilitate university studies for adults
- New teaching methods such as distance teaching, out-reach activities or work-related studies
- Utilization of adult students in programme design and course development

An Open Door Policy centers more on universities or colleges as such trying to change their attitudes, administrative routines and modes of teaching and learning. In contrast to this perspective, we can outline a *Policy of Recurrent education*, which aims at a total reorganization of the educational system. Typical for a policy of recurrent education is:

- A strong focus on the organizational interaction between different institutions of post-compulsory education (e.g. upper secondary schools, schools for adults, higher education) in order to broaden the population of prospective students in higher education, and, also, by providing necessary subject knowledge for further learning activities.
- An effort to provide a variety of educational routes through formal and non-formal learning settings, and not stressing the idea that higher education is the ultimate goal of each learning activity.
- An interest in organizational adaptation and curriculum development that can meet the needs of more heterogeneous student groups and not only adults.
- A special attention towards the interaction between higher education and working life on the one hand and social and financial support mechanisms on the other

A main part of the discussion at conferences on adults at university and college level emanates from the first perspective. This is most significant for countries with a rather low level of participation of adults in higher education. In Sweden, with a comparatively high level of adult participation, we are facing another kind of discussion. It is not the question of an adult minority of adults in isolation surrounded by masses of young students, Rather, it has up to the beginning of the eighties been an adult majority, with in fact rather limited influence on curriculum structure and educational content. Thus, it is easy to see that the situation, which might be described as 'post-progressive' cannot be easily transformed to other countries with much lower levels of adult participation. Further, there is a marked difference between the idea of specific programmes and courses for adults and an integrated or unified higher education system.

Another, common question reflected in both policy perspectives is:

Who is the adult student?

An alternative way of formulating the question is: Are we aiming at the right kind of adult students? As has been shown in the Swedish case study, higher education is not an efficient tool to reach out to underprivileged adults in different life or work settings. Undoubtedly, there is much to do in order to counteract the social bias of higher education. On the other hand, we must also ask what higher education can do for underprivileged people? To what extent can they benefit from higher learning and to what extent are other forms of adult studies more useful in their specific context? It is not our purpose to legitimate the social bias of higher education, rather it is necessary to stress the opinion that higher education cannot always be the ultimate goal of each learning acitivity. Other channels of knowledge and experiential sharing in a Swedish setting are folk high schools and study circles, municipal adult education, labour market training, staff development programmes, massmedia and self-directed learning. In such a context, studies at higher education level represents a more long-term strategy for the individual.

As a final remark, we hope, that the report has pointed to some general policy issues related to adult higher education in Sweden. Without any ambitions of presenting a summary of these issues, we would like to mention the following problems:

• What is meant by an adult student – what are the pros and cons of integrated and separated systems for educating young and adult students? To what extent can one develop different forms of educational differentiation within an integrated system?

• How can we develop adult study support schemes that integrate study finance, educational leave and counselling? Should we give these schemes a more selective character as far as adult higher education is concerned? And, most, important, who pays? The state, the student, or the employer? And, who pays for those who are not employed or want to broaden their minds?

• Would Sweden benefit from increased use of individual assessment and diagnostic approaches in the introductory process?

• To what extent are the Swedish problems in meeting the needs of the working adult a reflection of too rigid a programme structure? To what extent can Sweden benefit from the recognition of prior experience-models where a good combination between professional experiences and subject knowledge is an objective?

• To what extent can the idea of local study programmes be used as an innovative tool to meet the technological challenge; how can we overcome the obstacles of budget cuts in a state financed system of higher education? Under what conditions can the restrictive financial situation be an innovative force, and when is it just an obstacle?

• What are the risks and challenges involved in introducing commissioned higher education on a larger scale? When can such an approach be combined with separate courses already provided?

• What kind of subject-related and other qualifications are necessary for teachers and supervisors in adult higher education? And how can different programmes of staff development be designed in order to improve teaching capacity and the adjustment to the needs and social context of more heterogeneous student groups?

• What are the incentives for staff development in a state financed system of higher education, what is the cost-benefit equation seen from the individual teacher's point of view?

• What kind of balance between broader perspectives and common learning on the one hand and up-grading professional skill on the other is to be sought? Is there really a contradiction between broader perspectives and professional competence? How can we define the component of critical thinking in professional competence? What consequences of curriculum structure and educational design can be drawn from different ways of recognizing this balance?

• Is age an interesting and constructive criterion for different kinds of educational adaptations or adjustments? The answer must be no; it is not possible to develop an educational setting only in relation to age. We must also take other characteristics into consideration; e.g. study motives and learning attitudes, prior subject knowledge and study skill, social conditions and life setting, professional background and current work context.

To sum up: Swedish adult higher education has passed through a fascinating development and transformation during the last century. Its roots go back to the British University-Extension movement at the end of the 19th century and also the idea of self-education stressed by the early Swedish popular movements. It was a time when adult students formed a small, almost non-existing minority, at our universities. This low level of adult participation characterizes Swedish higher education up to the fifties or the early sixties, when Sweden witnessed a dramatic rise of adults in higher education. Today, over a hundred years after the active years of our educational ancestors, Swedish higher education comprises an adult majority in many degree-programmes and most separate courses. The process of "adultification" develops parallel to a general expansion of the Swedish educational system, and followed by a broader provision of educational opportunities in higher education. This change has not, however, led to a more effective recruitment of educationally under-privileged students. Does this fact lead us to the conclusion that the reform-strategy has been a failure? The answer is no. A policy of recurrent education cannot focus only on Open Door measures at universities and colleges. It also has to create policy concepts and instruments stressing the need for an effective interaction between upper secondary schooling, adult education and higher education. This is not an easy task, a problem that could be solved once and for all. It is a permanent challenge. Therefore, Swedish adult higher education must cope with new and strategic problems in the future.

• What consequences will the evaluation of the adult education reforms have on higher education?
• How can the admission system be reformed in order to strengthen the interaction between upper secondary schooling, adult education and higher education, taking the idea of recurrent education into consideration?
• What consequences will renewal funds and an increasing amount of commissioned higher education have on the programme structure, subject content and recruitment pattern?

# Notes

Chapter 1

1  See Abrahamsson, K. (1982a) "Prior experiences in higher education" in
   *International Encyclopedia of Education: Research and Studies*, Pergamon Press
   1984 and Abrahamsson, K. (1982b) *"Cooperative education, experiential
   learning and personal knowledge"* UHÄ-rapport 1982:1 National Board of
   Universities and Colleges, Stockholm. A research programme on these
   issues is presented by Wagner, A. (1981) "A research agenda for RPL-
   programs", in Abrahamsson (1982b).

2  The Klagenfurt seminar held November 3-5, 1982 and the Swedish presen-
   tations included a paper by Abrahamsson, K. (1982) *"From Extramural
   Studies to an Integrated System of Higher Education"* and a paper by Linné,
   *"Content, Curriculum and Work Experience – Aspects of Educational
   Integration in Higher Education Programs".*

3  For more detailed information on the Swedish admission policy, see
   Kim, L. (1982) *Widened Admission to Higher Education in Sweden – The 25/5-
   scheme. A study of the Implementation Process,* Studies in Higher Education in
   Sweden, NBUC. The Swedish work experience policy is also reported in
   Abrahamsson, K., Kim, L. & Rubenson, K. (1980) *"The value of work
   experience in higher education"* Reports on Education and Psychology No 2/1980.
   Stockholm Institute of Education, Department of Educational Research.

4  See *Direktiv 1983:58 Översyn av reglerna för tillträde till grundläggande högskoleutbildning* The main tasks for this commission has been to evaluate the
   admission system as a whole, and to suggest necessary technical modifications of the admission system in order to improve the balance between
   young and old students, to discuss the question of relevant work experience

in the admission process. Two other objectives are to analyze the requirements of certain subject knowledge in different programmes and to pay special attention to the need for admission tests in Swedish higher education. Thus, the commission can be seen as an expression of a need to deal with the vague and relatively open definitions of entrance requirements, that characterized Swedish higher education policy during the seventies. See also the recently published final report *"Tillträde till högskolan"*, SOU 1985:57.

5   See Kim, L. (1983)*Att välja eller väljas. En studie av tillträdesreglerna och övergången från gymnasieskola till högskola* UHÄ/FoU Projektrapport 1983:4

6   See Abrahamsson, K. & Rubenson, K. (1981) *Higher education and the "lost generation" - some comments on adult students, knowledge, ideals and educational design in Swedish post-secondary education* a paper presented at the IMHE workshop on "Meeting the demands of the adult population: a challenge for management", CERI/OECD, Paris May 1981, and
Svensson, A. (1981) *Jämlikhet i högskolan - fiktion eller verklighet? Den sociala rekryteringen till högre utbildning före och efter högskolereformen,*UHÄ-rapport 1981:25, and
Reuterberg, S-E & Svensson A. (1983) *Studiemedel som rekryteringsinstrument och finansieringskälla. Förändringar under 70-talet enligt de studerandes bedömningar* UHÄ/FoU Projektrapport 1983:1.

7   See Government Bill of the fiscal year of 1982/83; *Prop 1982/83:100;* Enclosure 10, pages 376-377.


Chapter 2

1   Olsson, O. (1925) *Universiteten och det svenska folkbildningsarbetet* Stockholm, Hugo Gebers förlag.

2   See Lindberg, B. (1980) Från prästskola till högskola, in: *17 uppsatser i svensk idé- och lärdomshistoria* Uppsala, Bokförlaget Carmina.

3   See Johannison, K. (1980) Svensk upplysningstid, in: *17 uppsatser i svensk idé- och lärdomshistoria* Uppsala, Bokförlaget Carmina.

4   For more detailed information on the Swedish admission policy, see Kim, L. (1982) *Widened Admission to Higher Education in Sweden - The 25/5-scheme. A Study of the Implementation Process,* Studies in Higher Education in Sweden (Stockholm, National Board of Universities and Colleges); see also Abrahamsson, K. (1982a) *From extramural studies to an integrated system of higher education - the adult student in retrospect* (conference paper, Stockholm, National Board of Universities and Colleges).
For a description of the general reform objectives see
Abrahamsson, K., Kim, L. & Rubenson, K (1980) *"The value of work experience in higher education"* Reports on Education and Psychology

No 2/1980. Stockholm Institute of Education, Department of Educational Research.

Dahllöf, U. (1977) *Reforming higher education and external studies in Sweden and Australia* Uppsala Studies in Education 3. Uppsala: Acta Universitatis Upsaliensis/Almqvist & Wiksell International.

Premfors, R. (1980) *The politics in higher education in a comparative perspective* Stockholm: Department of political science, University of Stockholm

5  The idea of phased exits of general study programmes has to some extent been analyzed by Rubenson in a project on recurrent education in Swedish higher education. See Rubenson, K. (1979) *Högskolans anpassning till återkommande utbildning – förutsättningar inom och utom systemet* UHÄ-rapport 1979:1. The problem is also discussed in Abrahamsson, K. & Rubenson, K. (1981) *Higher education and the 'lost generation'*

6  See Dahllöf, U. (1983) *An educational magpie: a case study about student flow analysis and target groups for higher education reform in Sweden* a paper presented at the NBUC conference "Studies of Higher Education and Research Organization", Dalarö, Sweden, June 1983.

7  See Kim, L. (1982) *Widened Admission to Higher Education in Sweden – The 25/5-scheme. A Study of the Implementation Process*, Studies in Higher Education in Sweden, NBUC.

8  The parliament commission on the evaluation of the reform did not publish a final report. Problems related to educational design and programme structure have been analyzed in a project by Agneta Bladh, (1981) *The trends towards towards vocationalism in Swedish higher education* Report 21, Group for the Study of Higher Education and Research Policy, Department of Political Science, University of Stockholm. Bladh has also published four reports in Swedish: (1981) *Enstaka kurser i högskolan*, UHÄ-rapport 1981:26; (1982) *Linjeutbildning i högskolan*, UHÄ-rapport 1982:25 and (1983) *De studerande och studieorganisationen. Uppföljningsundersökningar 1977-1982* UHÄ/FoU, Projektrapport 1983:2. Further, a discussion report has been published *På rätt kurs i högskolan. Erfarenheter av högskolans studieorganisation* UHÄ/FoU skriftserie 1983:4.

9  Bauer, M. *The UHÄ programme for the follow-up of the reform of higher education – current status* R&D for higher education, 1979:7. A list of the main reports of the evaluation programme is presented in Informationsblad 1983:8 of the new programme of evaluation and policy studies (Uppföljning & policystudier), NBUC.

10  This is, of course, a provocative statement, taking into consideration that the reform evaluation programme has resulted in over 50 reports and books. An important part of the programme has been dealing with the institutional structure and forms of public influence, the budget system and activity evaluation and also different aspects of the admission system and the selection process. The studies on programme structure and

educational design have primarily analyzed the provision of courses and programmes and not drop out and study results. My own research has mainly been oriented towards knowledge definitions and learning perspectives of Swedish adult higher education.

11 The changing reform pattern does not only include higher education, but also the compulsory school and the system of upper secondary education. In the latter case, the government presented a new bill in March 1984 aiming at a reform of the whole system of upper secondary education. The main content of this bill is not a new set of rules and a new organizational structure, but a mandate for regional and local authorities to initiate experiments and local educational development, thereby starting the reform process from the bottom-up rather than from the top-down.

12 The problems have been discussed at different seminars, but yet not resulted in joint projects. See Abrahamsson, K. (1982, ed.) *Högskola, arbetslivsanknytning och kunskapssyn. En diskussionsrapport om yrkesinriktning och bildningssyn i högskoleutbildningen* UHÄ and two recently published books on the ideas of higher education Abrahamsson, K. (1984, ed.) *Bildningssyn och utbildningsreformer.* UHÄ/Liber Utbildningsförlaget and Abrahamsson, K. (1985, ed.) *Högskolans bildningsprogram – finns det?* UHÄ/FOU Skriftserie 1985:2.

13 See Abrahamsson, K. (1982) *From extramural studies to an integrated system of higher education – the adult student in retrospect* Conference paper NBUC.


Chapter 3

1 See SCB (1980) *Trender och prognoser* IFP 1980:4

2 SCB (1983) *"Studerandes ålder 1981"* Statistiska meddelanden U 1983:13, page 24.

3 See BASFAKTA om högskolans anslag, utbud och rekrytering 982/83. Arbetssrapport från utredningssektionen, 1985. UHÄ.

4 See note 2 above.

5 See SCB (1983) *Siffror om högskolan 1: Rekryteringen till högskolan 1977/78-1980/81,* page 19.

6 SCB (1983) *"Studerandes ålder 1981"*. See note 3 above.

7 UKÄ (1976) *Nya studerandegrupper vid filosofisk fakultet. 1. Preliminär resultatredovisning* UKÄ/SCB, page 26.

8 See SCB (1983) note 5 above, page 25.

9 See Abrahamsson, K. & Rubenson, K. (1981) *Higher education and the 'lost generation'* note 6, Chpt 1 above.

10 SCB (1980) *Trender och prognoser* IFP 1980:3.

11 See Kim, L. (1983) *Att välja eller väljas. En studie av tillträdesreglerna och övergången från gymnasieskola till högskola* UHÄ/FoU Projektrapport 1983:4.

Chapter 4

1 See SCB (1981) *"Social skiktning i grundskola, gymnasieskola och högskola"* Information i prognosfrågor 1981:3, page 59.

2 See Löfgren, J. (1982) *Yrkesverksamhet efter avslutad yrkesteknisk högskoleutbildning* Pedagogisk forskning i Uppsala nr 35, 1982.

3 See Dominique, E. (1982) *Sjuksköterskor i förkortad läkarutbildning – de tre första studieåren* Karolinska institutet.

4 See Abrahamsson, K. & Rubenson, K. (1980) *Higher education and the 'lost generation'.* Conference paper, NBUC.

5 See Lindström, I. (1983) *Återkommande utbildning och högskolans yrkesinriktning. En fallstudie i Umeåregionen* UHÄ-rapport 1983:1

6 See *Prop 1975:9.*

7 See Bladh, A. (1983) *De studerande och studieorganisationen. Uppföljningsundersökningar 1977-1982* UHÄ/FoU Projektrapport 1983:2.

8 Some of these studies are referred in Abrahamsson, K. (1982) *Vad är den goda erfarenheten värd? Om relevant arbetslivserfarenhet i den nya högskolan* UHÄ-rapport 1982:11. Liber Utbildningsförlaget.

9 See Abrahamsson, K. (1982, ed.) *Vad är den goda erfarenheten värd?* and Abrahamsson, K., Kim, L. & Rubenson, K. (1981) *The value of work experience in higher education.*

Chapter 5

1 UHÄ-rapport 1983:17. Anslagsframställning för budgetåret 1984/85.

2 The idea of commissioned higher education programmes is discussed by Klintberg, W. (1983) in Furumark, A-M & Wahlén, S. (1983, eds) *Högskolan under omprövning. Fjorton debattinläg om högskolan i den ekonomiska krisen* UHÄ/FoU Skriftserie 1983/3 and by the governmental commission on education and productivity, see *Utbildning för framtid. Slutrapport från den utbildningsekonomiska utredningen* Ds U 1983:9. Furthermore, it must be added that the Swedish government presented a bill on commissioned adult and higher education in March, 1985.

3   This part is to some extent quoted from Abrahamson, K. & Rubenson, K. (1981) *Higher education and the 'lost generation'* and is originally from the report Högskoleutbildning i Stockholmsregionen 3/81. *Förslag till handlingsprogram för enstaka kurser och linjer.*

4   See Abrahamsson, K. & Rubenson, K. (1981) *Higher education and the 'lost generation'.*

5   See *prop* 1980/81:100 and *prop* 1980/81:20.

6   See *prop* 1980/81:20.

7   See Bladh, A. (1983) *De studerande och studieorganisationen. Uppföljningsundersökningar 1977-1982* UHÄ/FoU Projektrapport 1983:2.

8   See *Distansundervisning. Lägesbeskrivning samt organisatoriska alternativ för högskolan* TRU-kommittén, SOU 1975:72.

9   See *Distansundervisning i högskolan. Inriktning och utvecklingsmöjligheter* Rapport och förslag från regionstyrelsernas arbetsgrupp för distansutbildning, Umeå 1983.

10  See Willén, B. (1981) *Distance education at Swedish universities* Uppsala Studies in Education 16. Uppsala: Acta Universitatis Upsaliensis/Almqvist & Wiksell International, and Dahllöf, U., et al, *Evaluation, recurrent education and higher education reform in Sweden* Uppsala reports on Education, No 6.

11  See Abrahamsson, K. (1982) *From extramural studies to an integrated system of higher education - the adult student in retrospect* Conference paper, R&D-unit, NBUC.

12  See Pu-enheten, Lunds universitet; *Forskningscirkel Rapport från en konferens om fackliga forskningscirklar vid Lunds universitet,* 1983-05-27.


Chapter 6

1   See Abrahamsson, K. (1982) *From extramural studies to an integrated system of higher education - the adult student in retrospect* Conference paper, NBUC, and Abrahamsson, K. & Rubenson, K. (1981) *Higher education and the 'lost generation'. Comments on adult students, knowledge ideals and educational design in Swedish post-secondary education* Conference paper, NBUC/CERI/OECD.

2   The society of common civic knowledge and the information brochure *Läsning för folket* has been described by Sörbom, P. (1972) *Läsning för folket. Studier i tidig svensk folkbildningshistoria* Norstedt & Söner. The first 'bildungs'-circles have been investigated by Landelius, C. (1936) *1840- och 1850-talets bildningscirklar och arbetarföreningar i Sverige* Stockholm. The history of the idea of Workers' Institute has been studied by Leander, S. (1980) *Folkbildningens födelse. Anton Nyström och Stockholms arbetarinstitut 1880-1980* Nordiska muséet, Stockholm.

3  See SCB (1983) *De studerandes ålder 1981* Statistiska meddelanden U 1983:13, page 5.

4  See SÖ (1983) *Långtidsbedömningen (LB 83) avseende planeringsperioden 1984/85-1988/89.* Del I: Utvecklingslinjer, and Del II: Kvantitativ utveckling and SÖ (1984) *Långtidsbedömningen 1984 avseende planeringsperioden 1985/86 - 1989/90.*

5  The educational and administrative consequences of the new system of resource allocation to the independent educational associations is the subject of a specific case study. The main focus of this project is to analyze regional and local educational administrators' images of the functions of the new system. The results will later on be discussed in the context of broader surveys of social recruitment to adult education and study circles.

6  For a current description of the development of the system of municipal adult education; see Jacobsson, B. (1983) *KOMVUX enligt l-vux 82* SÖ.

7  See *Läroplan för kommunal vuxenutbildning. L-vux 82. Allmän del. Mål och riktlinjer. Timplaner. Kursplaner* SÖ 1983, pages 20-21.

8  See SOU 1983:22 *Utbildning för arbetslivet. Betänkande av kommittén för arbets-marknadsutbildning och företagsutbildning* (KAFU).

9  The changing educational traditions in the Swedish system of upper secondary schooling and higher education is analyzed in two books, see Abrahamsson, K. (1984, ed.) *Bildningssyn och utbildningsreformer. Om behovet av bildningsmål i gymnasium och högskola* UHÄ, Liber Utbildningsförlaget and Abrahamsson, K. (1985, ed.) *Högskolans bildningsprogram – finns det?* UHÄ/FOU Skriftserie 1985:2.

10  A new proposal of computer education for adults is discussed in Abrahamsson, K. (1985, ed.) *Datautbildning för alla vuxna.* Arbetsrapport 4, Forum för vuxenutbildningsdebatt.

11  See *Vuxenutbildning. 1970-talets reformer – en utvärdering.* Ds U 1985:10.


Chapter 7

1  This chapter is to a large extent built on the paper *Swedish post compulsory education in transition*, which was presented at a CERI/OECD-seminar on The participation of adults in higher education, Dublin, October, 1984.

2  See prop 1983/84:116 *Gymnasieskola i utveckling*, page 10.

3  See *Skolväsendet och vuxenutbildningen. Långtidsbedömning (LB 84) avseende planeringsperioden 1985/86 – 1989/90.* Skolöverstyrelsen, Stockholm 1984, page 32.

4  See note 3 above, page 34.

5  See note 2 above, page 12.

6　The quotation is from the upper secondary school bill, see note 2 above, and it reflects an important policy issue in the development of the Swedish system of post compulsory education.

7　Some of these issues are discussed in:
Abrahamsson, K. (red; 1982) *Vad är den goda erfarenheten värd? Om "relevant" arbetslivserfarenhet i den nya högskolan.* UHÄ-rapport 1982:11, Utbildningsförlaget Liber.
Abrahamsson, K. (red; 1984) *Bildningssyn och utbildningsreformer. Om behovet av bildningsmål i gymnasium och högskola.* Utbildningsförlaget Liber.
Abrahamsson, K. (1985, ed.) *Högskolans bildningsprogram – finns det?* UHÄ/FoU skriftserie 1985:2.


Chapter 8

1　See two other publications in this series, i.e. Begendal, G. (1983, ed.) *Knowledge and higher education. A series of colloquia* Studies in higher education in Sweden No: 2 and Bergendal, G. (1984, ed.) *Knowledge policy and knowledge traditions on higher education* Studies in higher education No. 6. NBUC, Almqvist & Wiksell International. Knowledge traditions in higher education are also discussed in Abrahamsson, K. (1984) *Bildningssyn och utbildningsreformer*, note 9, Chpt 6.

2　See Reuterswärd, A. *Yrkeskunnande och upplärning i industriföretag – en studie av rekryteringsproblem och möjligheter at lösa dem* Data- och elektronikkommittén. Ds I 1983:3.

3　See *Yrkeskunnande och upplärning i industriföretag*, summarized tables pages 40 and 42.

4　See Drambo, L. *Effekter av ny teknik på produktivitet, sysselsättning och arbetstid. En sekretariatsrapport från dataeffektutredningen* Ds A 1983:1, and Drambo, L. and Bark, A. *Kontorsautomation och kvinnors framtida arbetsmarknad. En sekretariatsrapport från dataeffektutredningen* Ds A 1983:9. Some of the general trends of the Swedish structural and technological transition is discussed in Abrahamsson, K. (1984) *Vuxenutbildning, strukturomvandling och sysselsättning* Arbetsrapport 1/84, Forum för vuxenutbildningsdebatt, Stockholm, and also arbetsrapport 4: *Datautbildning för alla vuxna.*

5　See *Utbildning för framtid. Slutrapport från utbildningsekonomiska utredningen* Ds U 1983:9.

6　See Adler, M. (1982) *The Paideia proposal. An educational manifesto* Macmillan publishing Co. Inc.

7　The quest for liberal learning perspectives are raised in Abrahamsson, K. (1984, ed.) *Bildningssyn och utbildningsreformer.* An interesting approach to a core curriculum in the humanities has been proposed by Duquid, S. (1983) *Humanities core curriculum. Human nature and human condition. Curriculum Guide*

Institute for humanities, Simon Fraser University, B.C.. The dilemma of balancing vocational orientation and the need for more 'educated' perspectives has been discussed by Harold Entwistle in different books, e.g. *Class, culture and education* Methuen, London 1978. Perspectives related to liberal education and general education are also discussed in Levine, A. (1981, ed.) *Common Learning. A Carnegie Colloquium on General Education*,The Carnegie Commission for the advancement of teaching.

8  This part is mainly borrowed from Abrahamsson, K. (1984) Does the Adult Majority Create New Patterns of Student Life? Some experiences of Swedish higher education *European Journal of Education, Vol. 19, No. 3, 1984.*

9  See Trow, M. (1974) "Problems in the transition from elite higher education to mass higher education", in *Policies for Higher Education* OECD, Paris.

# Appendix 1

## Swedish post-compulsory education in transition
## – a summary

Swedish post-compulsory education has been facing a situation of almost permanent transition since the late sixties. Reform ideas and new organizational structures have been implemented both in adult and higher education. Starting with universities and colleges, one important measure was the widening of access to higher education in 1969 and the provision of shorter vocational courses and study programmes in the beginning of the seventies. The Swedish Open Door policy (including the policy of crediting life and work experience) were, together with a strong working-life orientation of general study programmes and separate courses, two important parts of the reform of higher education of 1977. Another crucial aspect of the reform of universities and colleges was the creation of a new and integrated organizational structure for all higher education and conferment of higher educational status on a number of formerly non-academic programmes. One of the reform objectives behind this organizational transformation was to make the new system contribute to a more effective interaction with working life and also to support the idea of recurrent education.

Parallel to the reform of higher education, the Swedish parliament also decided to change the objectives, organizational structure and content of adult education. It is important to stress that the reforms in this area contained further support for Swedish popular adult education at folk high schools and study circles as well as the creation of a new adult education organization. Starting in 1967, a new system of so-called municipal adult education (komvux) was developed. These new adult education schools were to provide courses at secondary and upper-secondary school level for individuals who had not been able to continue their studies at a younger age.

One or two years after its implementation, this new organization was subjected to criticism, mainly from the big trade unions LO and TCO (the Swedish Trade Union Confederation and the Organization of Salaried Employees respectively). The critics felt that the new adult education schools (komvux) were too similar, to the educational ideas of the compulsory schools, thereby neglecting the adults' own experiences and social situations. Further, the critics undelined that the adult education schools were not reaching underprivileged groups in society. As a consequence, the government radicalized the objectives of these schools by giving them a broader social profile as part of the general goal of educational equality.

The reform in the adult education sector also included the law in 1975 of educational leave of absence and a new system of study finance for adults. New study support schemes were created both for underprivileged adults taking part in longer programmes, and for adults working and studying on a daily or hourly basis. The latter form of financial support was mainly intended to facilitate adult participation in study circles and other learning projects at locations close to the job. Another important component of the adult education reform strategy was an effort to develop new methods of out-reach activities both in working life and in the everyday life of adults.

Looking back on Swedish policy, it is easy to see that the seventies were the decade of adult and higher education. Today, in the mid-eighties, we have been facing a shift in policy ideas and priorities. Economic stagnation and government spending cuts, together with the threat of increasing youth unemployment, have led to increasing policy interest in education for young people. The new policy aims at a better balance between young and adult students. Different policy measures have been implemented at higher and upper secondary level. Let us start with decisions concerning higher education. Apart from the modification of the admission system with "better opportunities" for young students, there has also been an increase in the total number of available students places, mainly for young students at degree level. The general idea has been to give the young students of the eighties, comparable opportunities, as young students of the mid-seventies.

Another sign of the development is the strong political interest in a new reform and development programme for Swedish upper secondary education (gymnasieskolan). During the next five years, we are expecting a number of field experiments and development activities within upper secondary education where both study-oriented and vocationally directed programmes are concerned. The government has given special attention to four development areas viz a more flexible and adaptive organization of upper secondary schooling (gymnasieskolan), a better learning environment for the students, a stronger focus on subject-related job experience and field work as part of the learning process, and finally, a better interplay between upper secondary education and adult education, mainly the schools of municipal adult education.

The idea of recurrent education is one of the general objectives behind this new development scheme within upper secondary education. One point of departure for the reform work is that the general profile of the so-called theoretical programmes and the vocational programmes will be unchanged. Within this policy context, different organizational instruments will be developed in order to facilitate potential changes from a theoretical line to a vocational or vice versa. Thus, a number of "bridging courses" will be developed in order to provide a broader working life orientation for students taking theoretical lines and to give students taking vocational lines options for further studies. The purpose of these measures is to make different programmes more equal where vocational and educational goals are concerned. Another important part of the reform of upper secondary schools is a governmental task force on the shorter vocational programmes with the Swedish gymnasieskola. One of the main issues of this task force is to develop different models of interaction between vocational programmes and working life; i.e. different programmes of cooperative education.

If we combine the adult and higher education reforms of the seventies with the new reform strategy for upper secondary schools in the mid-eighties, we will have reached a new scenario for implementing the idea of recurrent education in Sweden. The new adult education curriculum within the schools of municipal adult education, starting from the 1981/82 fiscal year, is another important measure in a system of recurrent education. Thus, both in terms of principle and organizationally speaking, we can see a second chance for the idea of recurrent education. It is a common experience, however, that constructive innovations and development schemes cost more money than regular routine activities. This is also true for the future life of the idea of recurrent education.

Faced with the clamp-down on government spending, many politicians and also civil servants have, up to now, given priority to youth education before adult education; or to be more specific: the policy attention is focussed on educational structures between the traditional areas of compulsory schools and adult education. Further, the fiscal crisis favours selective admission strategies instead of compensatory educational strategies for those who have been admitted. Thirdly, the financial support for adult students does not make up for their reduced incomes or lost salaries. It is difficult, however, for the government to find money in order to increase the level of the grants or the total volume of the study support schemes. Recently, the government proposed a more differentiated structure for the Swedish system of study loans and study grants

It has also to be mentioned that the government recently introduced a Bill "renewal funds", i.e. education funds created from 10 % of the profits of successful industries and commercial enterprises. It is then up to trade unions and employers to negotiate how to use these funds for research, development and adult staff development and vocationally oriented forms of adult education.

When the Swedish Parliament in December 1984 accepted this Bill, it certainly opened up a new resource channel for Swedish adult education.

To sum up: Swedish post-compulsory education has undergone a number of changes in the last two decades. The next five or ten years do not seem to reflect a steady state. The fact that almost all young students tend to go to vocational or theoretical programmes in upper secondary education will, in the long run, raise new and challenging expectations in adult and higher education. Some of these policy issues ar reflected in two other current government Bills (No 1983/84:116 on a new system of upper secondary schools and No 1983/84:168 on municipal adult education) of 1984. Further, the government has also prepared an Adult Education Bill and a policy discussion is in progress concerning a reform programme in computer skills and computer knowledge for all adult citizens. In addition, it has to be mentioned that there are two governmental commissions on issues related to adult and higher education.

The first task force is evaluating the Swedish adult education reform strategy during the seventies. The second commission is – as has been mentioned in the introductory chapter – analyzing the higher education admission process, including credits for work experience, subject marks and tests, and also a quota system for different kinds of applications to higher education. A crucial task of the latter commission is – in the policy context of recurrent education – to scrutinize the learning value and formal competence of studies in municipal adult education. It is easy to see that the Swedish Admission Commission has a very important function to fulfill concerning different alternatives of recurrent education. In addition to this anticipated development, it has to be mentioned that Parliament recently enacted a new commission on the organization of labour market training. The new organization, formally starting on January 1st, 1986, is supposed to be more flexible and responsive on behalf of curriculum development and educational design.

# Appendix 2

## The organization of Swedish higher education

### Educational structure and admission system

The 1975 Higher Education Act and the subsequent reform of 1977 established that all subsequent planning of the education system was to be based on recurrent education as a regular model for the individual's educational planning. Recurrent education became one of the overriding principles which was to permeate the entire higher education system. The reform strategy did not focus on ear-marked measures either for the promotion of recurrent education or for specific programmes or organizational solutions for adult students; instead these aims were to be achieved by means of various general organizational measures. The principle of a unitary system of higher education, in which all forms of post-secondary education were to be accomodated within a single organization and in principle to be governed by the same goals, furnished an external framework for the organizational solutions.[1]

The main premise of the planning process was that higher education should prepare students – although in a general way – for vocational activity in a particular sector of working life. Thus, the reform implied a substitution of the principle of knowledge organization in disciplines and subjects for a knowledge organization related to the following sectors of working life:

- technical professions
- medical and paramedical professions

- administrative, economic and social professions
- teaching professions
- cultural and communicative professions

The separate courses can be viewed as comprising a category in its own right, but it must be pointed out that the content of these courses also reflects the above areas.

Within this organizational context, the provision of general study programmes and separate courses at the undergraduate level by the colleges and universities were of four kinds:

- general full-degree programmes or general study lines
- local full-degree programmes or local study lines
- individual full-degree programmes or individual study lines and
- single or separate courses

The main purpose of the programmes is to provide higher education at the undergraduate level geared to the needs of the labour market and society. The essential purpose of the separate courses is that of providing subsequent and further training for persons already vocationally active. The final decision of the dimensioning and planning frames governing the allocation of resources for student places in different programmes is taken by the Riksdag (the Swedish Parliament), while the task of distributing funds for separate courses and for local and individual programmes was entrusted to the regional boards established in the reform.

Another essential feature of the reform was the geographical distribution of educational amenities. This was primarily arranged through the establishment of a number of small higher education colleges without earmarked resources for research. Mention must also be made of the distance teaching experiment and the extramural courses organized outside the university towns. In this respect the 1977 reform marked the culmination of an expansion of the higher education system as such. Another important feature of the new organization was the inclusion of a number of non-academic forms of education, nursing education and various forms of teacher training. With few exceptions, the unified Swedish system of higher education comprises all forms of post-secondary education.

The Swedish admission system makes a fundamental distinction between *general qualifications* (eligibility) and *special requirements*.

The admissions scheme defines four main ways of obtaining *general eligibility* for higher education. They are:

*1* to have completed a three-year stream of the upper secondary school
*2* to have completed a two-year stream of the upper secondary school

*3* to have the equivalent education from a 'folk high school'
*4* to have more than 4 years work experience and to be over 25 years of age (the 25:4 qualification).

In these admission rules work experience is given a wide interpretation; any kind of work experience including child care and military service can be included in the 4 years required for the 25:4-qualification. However, the *special requirements* often mean that the equivalent of upper secondary school knowledge of certain subjects is required in addition to the general requirements (which also include a knowledge of Swedish and English). On a voluntary basis, adult students can take a general aptitude test. One of the most radical parts of the reform was the introduction of work experience as an additional entrance merit for young students. This decision may in the long run contribute to an increased age-level in the system.

*Planning system and resource allocation*
Another important change was the establishment of new planning and decision-making bodies. At the central level, the former UKÄ, University Chancellor's Office, was reconstituted in 1976 as UHÄ or the National Board of Universities and Colleges (NBUC), thereby becoming the general planning authority for all post-secondary education. At the regional level, as has already been mentioned, six regional boards were set up. Their main task was to achieve a more concerted repertoire of educational amenities adapted to regional needs and also to promote co-operation between different universities and colleges. At the local level (i.e. university and college), a system of programme committees was set up to take charge of the planning and further development of general study programmes. Public representatives came to form a majority at the regional level, while university and college boards were dominated by teachers, researchers and other staff. The balance between different interests at different levels of the system was an issue in a discussion report published by the government during spring 1983.[2] (figure A2:1, page 90)

On a general level, it is easy to describe the system of resource allocation in Swedish higher education. As shown by Figure 1 above, all financial resources emanate from the state, and the allocation is formally taken as a decision in the Swedish Riksdag. Financial support for general degree-oriented programmes is distributed from the state level directly to universities and colleges, while the money for single or separate courses and, also, local study programmes is channelled through the regional boards.

Thus, the regional boards are expected to have an important policy

**Figure A2:1** Patterns of resource allocation in Swedish higher education

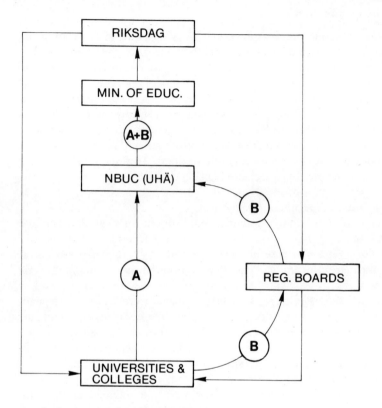

A = budget request for general programmes
B = budget request for sep. courses and local lines

function as far as continuing higher education is concerned. One of the main responsibilities of these boards, is to develop a functional balance between intramural and extramural higher education. The regional boards have the authority to decide on the proportion of separate courses, which should be distributed off-campus or as distance-courses. Further, they have the responsibility to accept or reject proposals of new local study programmes. The capacity of these regional boards to cope with their task has been subject to discussion during the last few years.[3]

The budget cycle at state level is divided into fiscal years. A new fiscal year starts on July 1 of one calendar year and continues until June 30, the next year. The universities and colleges as well as the regional boards send their budget proposals to the National Board of Universities and Colleges during the spring of the first year, and the NBUC analyses policies and priorities during April, May and June and presents its total request for financial support to the Minister of Education at the end of August (which is the beginning of the next fiscal year).

The policy formation of the new Education Bill takes place from September to December and the government usually presents the bill in mid-January and the Riksdag makes the decision in May of the second year, and thereby establishes the frames of the financial support for the following fiscal year (year 3): In addition to the formal process of written proposals from the local and regional level to the NBUC and the NBUC's proposal to the government, and the decision in the Riksdag, there is a continuous 'budget dialogue' going on between the NBUC and the local level and between the NBUC and the Minister of Education. As an example, the National Board is given the opportunity to read and comment on the Government Bill before it is printed and sent to the Riksdag. The same communication pattern is developed between the regional boards and the universities and colleges within each region.

The fact that Swedish higher education is totally state financed does not imply that the system is independent of market influence. The market expectations are reflected more through the student needs and choices than through the financial system. In contrast to some other countries, e.g. the USA, the students pay only a minor part of the educational costs. With the exception of a small registration fee, study material and listed books, the educational costs are covered by public money. The majority of students also have access to student loans, while grants are mainly available for basic adult education.

Despite these conditions, an adult student in a mid-career change may meet severe social and economic obstacles, when he or she embarks on a project of higher learning. The educational choice is to a large extent determined by what can be seen as occupationally useful and beneficial, especially if the mid-career student has to pay back his study loans during his remaining occupational years. Undoubtedly, adult students aiming at degree-oriented studies take decisions at a high risk-level.

Labour market demands and expectations are not only reflected through the students' choices, but also, and maybe to a more general extent, at the political level. One of the objectives of the reform of 1977 was to orient the system of higher education to problems of working life. Degree-oriented programmes are supposed to have a strong vocational component. The provision of separate courses is mainly oriented towards the needs of the occupationally active students. Thus, the political decision on the number of student places in various general study programmes and the profile of separate courses has to take developments in the labour market into account.[4]

## Renewal in the context of cut-backs

Like most western countries Sweden has been facing economic stagnation and financial crisis, something that not only stresses the need for a more efficient use of public money, but also various forms of cut-backs and a more restricted public policy. The cuts are not as dramatic as in some other countries. Swedish higher education authorities (i.e. regional boards and universities and colleges) have been told to reduce their costs by 2% per year for a period of five years. It is evident, however, that an even budget cut can have very selective effects on different programmes or educational sectors.[5]

From a policy point of view, this new development raises questions of how innovations can be initiated and implemented in times of retrenchment and cuts in public funding. It is often said that a more restrictive public policy and the threat of the elimination of certain programmes or courses could be an innovative tone in itself. In this respect, the new budget situation might have an innovative effect as far modifications of old programmes are concerned. It is doubtful, however, to what extent this principle is applicable for the development of new programmes and courses.

Let us take one example of this dilemma. The government policy is to restrict the provision of separate courses, and to increase the number of student places in degree-oriented programmes. To develop new courses or programmes costs more than keeping traditional programmes. An innovation in the field of separate courses might create certain financial problems in times of retrenchment and limited public budget. Some of the new separate courses provided (courses in the field of computers and micro-electronics could be taken as examples) are more expensive than separate courses in general. Thus, the idea of budget cuts as a challenge to innovations might influence the departments of higher education to develop a special market profile or a new curricular identity. The threat is, however, not so useful as far as new resources for innovations are concerned. The expectation of 'new resources', is discouraged, as can be seen from the following quote from the government bill of 1983/84:

As I have already remarked, the economic situation demands

extreme restraint in the matter of public spending. At the same time, a great deal of change and renewal will be needed in both research and education. In the latter sector, moreover, commitments will have to be honoured which have already been entered into with the aim of giving the large generations of young persons access to higher education and reforming certain types of education. Reforms will also be called for in subsequent years. All these things will have to be financed within unchanged financial frames. Rigorous demands will have to be made concerning the efficiency with which higher education resources are utilized. This being so, I propose to initiate a review of resource utilization within the higher education system. This review will not be aimed at revising the objectives or the general code of rules applying to higher education. Instead it will mainly be concerned with studying the way in which resources are utilized within the existing organization. For example, a study should be made of the size of teaching groups and the utilization of teaching personnel resources, departmental boundaries, the interaction between various higher education agencies, the budgeting process, personnel administration, accounting systems and other matters.

Government bill of education 1983/84, page 378

The development in Sweden calls for a more clarified discussion of the pros and cons of general and selective cut-backs in higher education. Further, it is necessary to analyze the impact of cut-backs on the teaching-learning level. And in addition it would be interesting to analyze to what extent the new budget situation will influence the participation level and educational conditions of adults in higher education? Finally, it is important to mention alternative forms of financial support in the Swedish system of higher education. Two examples may illustrate this issue. Firstly, there is an increasing amount of commissioned higher education programmes; i.e. organizations or enterprises buying target-designed programmes or courses. Secondly, the Parliament took a decision on renewal funds in December 1984, thereby transmitting parts of the corporate profits (10% if the profit exceeded 500 000 Sw.Kr.) to research, development or education.

# Notes

1 See Dahllöf, U. (1977) *Reforming higher education and external studies in Sweden and Australia* Uppsala Studies in Education 3. Uppsala: Acta Universitatis Upsaliensis/Almqvist & Wiksell International
Premfors, R. (1981) *Integrated higher education: The Swedish experience* Report 14, Group for the study of higher education and research policy. University of Stockholm.

2 See *Högskolans institutionella organisation* DsU 1983:6.

3 The discussion started in the reform process and has continued since then. See for example Dahllöf, U. & Willén, B. (1978) "Regional högskoleplanering – hot eller löfte?" In Abrahamsson, K. (1978, ed.) *Högskola för återkommande utbildning. En debattskrift från UHÄ:s grupp för återkommande utbildning* UHÄ-rapport 1978:20. The status of the regional boards was also a main issue of the reform evaluation commission that worked between 1979 and 1982. On the other hand, one can say that the regional boards have been actively involved in developing methods and networks for a better regional and local planning of post compulsory education in Sweden.

4 These problems have been discussed by a commission on education and productivity, see *Utbildning för framtid. Slutrapport från utbildningsekonomiska utredningen* DSU 1983:9

5 Problems of educational consequences of cut backs in higher education have been analyzed in a special project by Wahlén, S. (1983) *Pengar och kvalitet. En genomgång av utländsk litteratur om högskoleplanering i nedskärningstider* UHÄ/FoU Skriftserie 2:1983, and Wahlén, S. & Eklundh, P. (1983) *Mindre pengar – sämre utbildning. Några undersökningar av effekter av nedskärningar i grundutbildningen* UHÄ/FoU Projektrapport 1983:3. Objectives, obstacles and innovative methods of planning during financial restrictions or retrenchment have been articulated in a book edited by Furumark, A-M & Wahlén, S. (1983) *Högskolan under omprövning. Fjorton debattinlägg om högskolan i den ekonomiska krisen* UHÄ/FoU Skriftserie 1983:3.

# Appendix 3

Study support mechanisms: educational leave of absence study finance and counselling

### Educational leave and study finance

Social and financial support to adult students has a crucial function for the facilitation of recurrent education. In Sweden, educational leave and study finance are administered through two different systems. The Swedish Riksdag took a formal decision on a special law of educational leave, which came into effect at the beginning of 1975. This law entitles all public and private employees to leave their jobs for educational activities during shorter or longer periods. To qualify, the employee must have been working at the same firm or company at least six months consecutively or a total of twelve months during the previous two years.

The right to educational leave covers all types of education – general, vocational and trade union-oriented. The application of this law is subject to negotiations between employers and trade unions. the employers can not postpone an individual worker's right to educational leave more than six months. In other cases the employers have to make a special agreement with the local trade union. The Act does not consider how the studies will be financed, but it guarantees the employee the right to return to his job after his educational experience and also to resume the status and income he had beforehand.

The fact that the law of educational leave has not been coordinated with the system of study finance is an interesting research issue concerning the implementation of the idea of recurrent education. The Swedish way of not choosing a model of paid educational leave was a conscious reform strategy. The general argument was that a separated system would increase the amount of support and, also, widen the scope of possible programmes and courses.[1] The main source of study finance is a system of state loans and grants. If we exclude staff development and up-grading of work related skills organized or paid for by the employers and the further education of teachers in the school system, it is unusual that employers pay the educational costs of the adult students i.e. by permitting them to study during paid working hours. Thus, we find important differences compared to the USA and Japan where employers and big enterprises tend to be important sources of study finance. This form of economic support is, however, closely regulated by the employers, who also decide upon which programmes and courses are relevant to the needs of the job.

The state supported system of study finance in Sweden comprises three distinct forms of social and financial benefit for adult students. Labour market trainees receive a special *educational grant*, adult students with restricted educational experiences might get special *adult study assistance*, while there is a more general *study assistance scheme* for different categories of students in adult and higher education. The education grant from the Labour Market Board (AMS) and the special study assistance scheme, which are more favourable as far as the relation of grants/loans is concerned, are seldom or never used for adult higher education. Adult students aiming at degree-oriented studies in higher education can apply for general study assistance.[2] (table A3:1, page 97)

The scheme of general study assistance (loans and grants) was introduced in 1965. The main objectives were to compensate for social and geographical bias and also improve the general economic conditions of students in higher education. The loan-grant assistance can be awarded to students from 20 to 50 years of age taking part in higher studies according to the new organization of higher education. The possibilities of getting this financial support are very liberal for adult studies at upper secondary school level and for vocationally oriented and shorter programmes of higher education. It is also possible to receive this support for long-term post-secondary education. The main part of this loan-grant support (90%) consists of money which must be repaid. The size of the general study assistance is adjusted according to a cost of living index, the number of children the adult student has and whether the student has extra sources of income or capital. Although there are no formal barriers for adults to utilize the general study assistance scheme, there are psychological and economic obstacles relating

Table A3:1 Different forms of financing recurrent education

| | Folk high school, elementary and secondary schooling for adults | Higher ed. | Labour market training | Short term folk high school courses; adult education associations |
|---|---|---|---|---|
| Educational grants (AMS) | (x) | | x | |
| Loan-grant assistance scheme | x | x | | |
| Adult study assistance* | x | | | x |

*Adult study assistance is not given for higher education with the exception of 700 persons at post secondary vocational education (YTH). The adult study assistance also includes a special hourly and daily based financial support for short courses.

to the increased amount of money that has to be repaid during a limited period of working years.

We still lack sufficient knowledge about the combined impact of the law of educational leave and study finance system as far as adult participation in higher education is concerned. Some evidence indicates that it has had the strongest effect on basic adult education and on trade union education.[3] Further there are empirical results indicating that the study finance system has had a positive effect on the recruitment of working class children to higher education. Longitudinal studies of two generations born in 1948 and 1953 have registered an increase in the equal distribution of educational opportunity during the sixties, but a decrease and a more selective system during the seventies.[4]

According to the report by Svensson et.al. it is evident that the study assistance scheme exerted considerable influence upon the recruitment of students with working class background during the sixties. Students with general study assistance are also more successful in their studies (i.e. complete their studies up to the final examination) than students without such support. It is interesting and somewhat surprising that educational opportunities for young students have decreased during the decade of significant reorganization of higher education in Sweden. The Open Door policies introduced at the beginning of the seventies might have made the system more open for certain groups of students and more selective for others.[5]

Within the framework of Svensson's project a comparative study of the adult study assistance scheme and the traditional loan/grant-system is in progress. The first scheme was primarily intended for compensatory adult education. There is some evidence, however, that the traditional system could, at least in the short run, give the same economic return. The special adult study assistance tends to be more favourable for women than for men, partly depending on prior income. The number of students in Swedish higher education is about 200 000, and the majority take separate courses. Only students within a special vocational programme for technicians (the YTH-scheme) will get the special study assistance. The number of loans/-grants for higher studies in 1982/83 118 000 i.e. about 60% of the total student population. Unfortunately, there are no statistics on the utiliz-ation-level of degree-students and separate course students. It seems probable, however, that the second group combine part-time studies with work to a much higher extent.

It is obvious, that the study assistance scheme has maintained a compensatory function by influencing the recruitment of primarily young students with working class background. We know less about its impact on adult participation in higher education. The second objective, that of giving students an acceptable standard of living has been more difficult to realize. During the past few years we have had an increasing debate on problems of study finance. It is more common for the students to have to work parallel with their studies in order to earn the extra money needed for themselves or for their family. Part-time work and part-time studies could be a construc-tive solution for adult students, but it is almost impossible to cope with in degree oriented programmes.

The Swedish experiences call for a deeper analysis of different patterns of part-time work and part-time studies in higher education. Work-study programmes, as they are developed in the USA, could have certain educational advantages, but they can also cause study problems and increased conflicts and cross-pressure.[6] According to the study by Svens-son, students who had to work parallel with their studies were those who had also been delayed in their studies.[7] This is, however, not surprising when taking their restricted time budget into consideration. (table A3:2, page 99)

The Swedish study finance schemes have also been the subject of a government commission, which worked between 1975 and 1981. So far, the reports of this commission have not been a source of major reforms, where adult study assistance is concerned. In the summer of 1981 the government gave the commission formal instructions to finish its work by presenting

**Table A3:2**  Differences in examination between working and non-working students; comparison between sexes.

| | Faculties of arts and sciences | | | Other faculties | | |
| --- | --- | --- | --- | --- | --- | --- |
| | Men | Women | Total | Men | Women | Total |
| Non-working students | 42 | 36 | 39 | 68 | 89 | 77 |
| Working students | 29 | 19 | 25 | 55 | 78 | 63 |
| Difference | 13 | 17 | 14 | 13 | 11 | 14 |

empirical data on the economy and standard of living of students and the impact of the study finance scheme up to the beginning of the 80s. In contrast to other public commissions, there were no major final proposals presented on future reforms in this field. The explanation is quite simple. A new system of study assistance would be too expensive taking into account the economic stagnation and current crisis of state finance and public expenditures. The fact that today the system accounts for 6 billion Swedish kronor, is a sign as good as any. In spite of the restricted state budget, or maybe because of it, the government did recently take the initiative to a new public commission on study finance.[8]

The end of reform in this area, is of course disappointing to advocates of recurrent education who would see an integration of educational leave, study finance and study support as major tools of better interaction between work and education. The present study assistance scheme is – what grants are concerned – more oriented towards adult basic education, and gives only limited opportunities for adults wanting to enter degree-oriented programmes in higher education. In the latter case, the students either have to work parallel with their studies or borrow money from the state.

## Information and counselling for adults

Counselling as an organizational concept or a specific task in higher education is a relatively new phenomenon in Swedish higher education. The establishment of the first positions in this respect in 1969 is to be viewed against the background of the heavy expansion of higher education and the resultant demands for more efficient studies and faster student flows. Educational counsellors were above all expected to help students in the planning and conduct of their studies and to get in touch with those who had run into difficulties. Before very long, however, educational counsellors were also being asked to supply students with labour market information and vocational guidance, due to declining employment for graduates.[9]

There are today som 400 educational counsellors attached to universities and colleges in Sweden. The majority of them are on the staff of the various university departments, but there are also educational counsellors attached to the central administration and admission service of universities and colleges. A number of educational counsellors are also attached to general study programmes. This has been the rule for quite a long time at the schools of advanced technology and those of medicine. The main trait here is peer counselling, e.g. advising activities being conducted by students.

Educational counsellors at universities and colleges have usually not received any counsellor training before obtaining their appointments. Instead they acquire this knowledge through in-service training. In addition to educational counsellors, and working in close collaboration with them, there are social workers who are appointed by the student unions. They have therapeutic qualifications and deal with more profound or personal problems.

Where labour market information and pure vocational counselling on an individual basis are concerned, educational counsellors co-operate with vocational counsellors from the local employment offices. It should be observed, however, that contrary to the practice frequently occurring in the USA and Great Britain, Swedish higher educational counsellors are not involved in placement activities. There are no regular employment channels between universities and employers, and the responsibilities accepted by universities on behalf of students are mostly confined to the duration of studies.

How does the 'adultification' of Swedish higher education affect educational counselling? Among many other things, of course, it accentuates the question of how to reach prospective students. When recruitment mainly involved upper secondary students, we were able, at least theoretically, to reach them, because we knew where to find them – in school. It is more difficult to reach a diffuse target group such as 'prospective adult students'. Every autumn term there are some 150 000 applicants for study programmes (central admissions) and for short-term courses (direct admissions at university level). Prospective students might find our admissions system cumbersome and complicated and it is as usual the people with the most initiative, perseverance and time who manage to reach educational counsellors.

One problem of the Swedish system of central admission concerns the drop-out soon after the beginning of studies. Firstly, we must exclude "admitted students", who do not use their student place i.e. students who choose another programme or course. Secondly, there are the drop-outs who give up because of misapprehension of the content, difficulty and time consumption of education. This is true both for students coming straight from upper secondary school (though to a somewhat lesser extent) and adult students. Thus, students have not received the information or guidance they need to make an educational choice based on knowledge of the education itelf and of the demands and preconditions it involves in relation to their preferences and aptitudes.

To the adult student, who is often forced into total commitment involving not only himself but also his family, employment etc., a mistaken venture is often disastrous. It can also be disastrous for a young student, but as a general rule there is a wider margin of error in the latter case, and mistakes are usually easier to rectify in the case of a person with few social and geographical ties.

Information disseminated about higher education, therefore, cannot be confined to educational opportunities and rules of admission. It is no less vital to encourage prospective students, by means of individual counselling, group discussions and informal arrangements, to identify their own needs, preferences and interests. The need for more evaluatively penetrating and individually tailored guidance of this kind is naturally increased in a system where the student has to make one final decision on quite a comprehensive study package. It is no surprise that many adult students prefer a step to step oriented model in which they explore their way ahead via a number of contingent decisions instead of one final one.

A conceptual model for the analysis of counselling problems in adult higher education has been presented by Abrahamsson as part of an evaluation study of different forms of information and counselling for prospective adult students. The seed of an interest is often sown long before the student approaches the admission procedure. Thus, an evaluation of an information and counselling strategy must work both in short-term and long-term perspectives. It is not sufficient just to disseminate leaflets and brochures on educational opportunities and labour market trends hoping that the students will overcome the barriers to higher education through their own energy and interest.[10]

One of the crucial functions of a recruitment and introductory strategy must be to help the prospective students better to clarify their needs, plans and obstacles. Two cases studied in the above mentioned project were focused towards these problems. The first case was an evaluation of an experiment with an orientation course for prospective adult students in higher education. The second case concerned an effort to use the study circle as a method of adult counselling. One conclusion of this study on adult counselling in higher education was that there was a growing need for adult counselling, guidance and study preparation. Another conclusion was that there was a risk involved in overinforming prospective adult students. If the information activities are not coordinated with other study support schemes, they might cause more study problems rather than result in effective participation.

# Notes

1 For a general picture of the Swedish model of study finance, see Rubenson, K. (1981) *Financing recurrent education – the Swedish model* Working paper of the department of educational psychology, Stockholm Institute of Education. This chapter is to a large extent based on Rubenson's paper. Studies into problems of study financing have also been performed by Allan Svensson at the department of education, University of Göteborg, see Reuterberg, S-E & Svensson, A. (1983) *Studiemedel som rekryteringsinstrument och finansieringskälla. Förändringar under 70-talet enligt de studerandes bedömningar* UHÄ/FoU Projektrapport 1983:1.

2 The matrix emanates from Rubenson, K. (1981) see note 1 above.

3 See Öberg, S. (1983) *Vilka har fått timstudiestöd och dagstudiestöd och vad har utbildningen betytt för dem?* Rapporter CSN 1983:2. All applicants in the labour market education programme are guaranteed and educational grant. The special daily or hourly based grant is often combined with trade union studies.

4 See Reuterberg, S-E & Svensson, A. (1983), note 1 above.

5 The Swedish Council of Study Finance has not yet done any comparative studies of study patterns of students on general programmes and separate courses. The main priorities have concerned adult education and adult basic education.

6 In contrast to USA and Japan, Swedish employers do not seem to play a main role in study finance for working adults. A majority of Swedish adult students in higher education are combining their studies with work or other activities. It would not be surprising if the degree of parallel work also is increasing among young students, mainly as a consequence of diminishing economic output of the existing forms of study finance. See Lundqvist, O. (1983) *Studiestöd för vuxna. Trender i utvecklingen efter 1975 års vuxenutbildningsreform* Rapport 1983:3, pedagogiska institutionen, Göteborgs universitet.

7 The table emanates from Reuterberg, S-E & Svensson, A. (1983) page 43.

8 The governmental Bill, 1984, includes some minor modifications of the Study finance system, and especially concerning its compensatory function.

9 See Abrahamsson, K. & Berg, C. (1981) *The organizational limits to higher education counselling – the case of Sweden* Conference paper, NBUC.

10 See Abrahamsson, K. (1976) *The need for a dialogue. On the counselling needs of presumptive adult learners in higher education* Doctoral dissertation department of education, University of Stockholm.

# Appendix 4

## Participation of Adults in Higher Education Country Survey Document*

### Part One: Objectives and Scope of Survey, Definitions

#### I CERI Work on Adult Participation in Higher Education

In 1983 and 1984, CERI work in the field of Innovation in Higher Education will focus on three particular aspects of higher education for adults.

1 First, CERI will look into *financial and organizational policies for the participation of adults in higher education*; finance as the availability of some kind of financial support, and organization as the way in which studies are organized, e.g. the possibility of part-time attendance or distance learning must be considered as important factors influencing an adult's decision to enrol or not to enrol. Stated negatively, the absence of such support or such possibilities tend to constitute important barriers to adult participation. *Following Patricia Cross' classification* of such barriers as 'situational', 'instructional' and 'dispositional' (Patricia Cross, *Adults as Learners*, San Francisco (Jossey Bass), 1981), the focus will thus be on the former two, trying to identify the nature of these barriers and those policies and institutional practice aiming at overcoming, eliminating or reducing them. *Barriers* of this kind, which call for policies such as better financial support, study leave, part-time provision, child care facilities, *primarily* affect those *students aiming for a full higher education degree* (a

*This document is reproduced by the permission of CERI, OECD.

bachelor's degree or its equivalent – see discussion below). This might also be of importance, even if a lesser degree, for certain categories of adult students who enrol for continuing education without aiming for such a degree.

2 Secondly, CERI will look more closely into the *role the higher education sector plays in continuing education*. Since it can be assumed that only a minority of adults in higher education study towards a full degree, *the majority is enrolled in some form of continuing or further education*, programmes which may or may not be provided by separate departments (adult education, extra mural, university extension departments). Students enrolled in continuing education are doing so for a wide variety of purposes ranging from *personal enrichment* to *different career-oriented reasons*, and the institutional response to the different demands from various categories of adult students is highly variegated. In some of the Member countries, this type of provision for adult students has a long standing tradition (e.g. the US and the UK). In other countries this task has been, until very recently, primarily assumed by the adult education sector outside the higher education sector (e.g. the German speaking countries). But in these countries, too, universities and other higher education institutions are beginning to accomodate the demand for education programme by adults thus competing with the traditional adult education sector, professional associations, etc.

3 Thirdly, CERI will study various *forms of distance teaching*. Most prominently among these figure the Open University and its various off-springs which mark one of the most noticed and successful departures from traditional and campus-based forms of higher education. The importance of this kind of new provision of higher education can hardly be over-estimated with respect to adult participation and will probably further increase as new technologies, applied to distance teaching and self-instructed learning, are being developed and becoming more gene-rally accessible.

## II Objectives of the Survey

4 It is the objective of the survey to *collect country information* and data about the situation of adults in higher education, in order to assess current policies and practices, that affect adults' participation in higher education. Data and information will be sought with respect to:

- the number of adults enrolled in higher education and their distribution by sex, age, cultural or ethnic origin, socio-economic and employment status;

- fields and types of study;

- patterns of participation (full-time, part-time, distance learning etc.)

- the availability of, and eligibility for, financial support for adult students;

- admission criteria and practice.

5   The survey does not aim at attempting a comparative quantitative analysis of the country data and information thus collected; rather these will be used for an analysis of policies and practices followed by governmental authorities and higher education institutions. Such an analysis is aimed at identifying those policies and practices that appear to enhance and those that appear to hinder participation by adults in higher education activities.

6   The data thus collected will also serve as background material for an *assessement of what is currently happening in Member countries with respect to continuing education provided by higher education institutions.*


## III   Scope of the Survey, Definitions

7   In order to determine the scope of the study, it is necessary to agree on a number of definitions.

8   It is relatively easy to define what is meant by *adult* or *mature student.* Although legally speaking almost all students enrolled in higher education are adults, it is obvious that the scope of this study must be meaningfully limited to those students who are older than the traditional student group, i.e. those who enroll in direct continuation of their upper secondary studies. In order to make clear that the focus is on those students who have been out of education for a substantial amount of time and hence had some years of labour force experience (civilian or military) or, in the case of women, raising their children, the age of 25 years can stand as a meaningful and representative proxy. Thus responses should refer to *those aged 25 years or older* who, in the case of first degree students, begin their higher education. This should not rule out those who had a short spell of higher education before but dropped out and took their studies up again after this age – provided that a substantial time has elapsed since that initial spell of enrolment.

**9** It is more difficult to define what is meant by *higher education*. Post-secondary provision in Member countries is highly variegated, and it often is difficult to distinguish between higher education and post-secondary education. Besides this difficulty, *certain experts advising the Secretariat pointed out that any international comparison concerning adult participation would be distorted if the focus were exclusively on higher education* since in many countries it is traditional adult education institutions that provide the kind of courses and programmes which in other countries, without such a tradition, are being offered by higher education institutions.

**10** Although aware of this difficulty, the Secretariat is of the opinion that higher education, whatever the exact definition be in the different countries distinguishing it from the post-secondary education sector, is a sector with a special function within post-secondary provision. This is even true in countries where this distinction is not at once exactly clear or where such a distincinction has been abolished. For even in the countries where this is the case, universities and equivalent *higher education institutions* (e.g. the polytechnics in the UK, Technische Hochschulen in Germany) are ascribed a special role. *It is the adult student in this kind of institutions on whom the present study will focus*, although the forms of provision for adult learning and their respective importance will have to be taken into account when assessing policies and practice with respect to adult participation in higher education. Thus, higher education includes universities and equivalent institutions which provide formal higher education courses and which are entitled to award academic or state degrees, certificates or diplomas.

**11** When attempting to survey the situation both full degree programmes and continuing education activities, it is obvious that the *definition of what kind of courses, programmes and activities are to be included* is of critical importance. Given the very different nature of degree programmes and educational offerings for continuing education students, it is appropriate to *distinguish two separate parts of the survey* (see below part two, chapters A and B). This distinction is reflected in two definition which, however, have a number of common elements.

**12** With respect to those courses which lead to and are creditable towards a full academic or state degree (to be reported according to part two, Chapter A, *higher education courses* are defined as courses

    a   which require *application, admission* (including open admission) *and registration*;

b    which *qualify for public funding* (through institutional support, student support or tax deduction);

d    the successful completion of which is formally recognized through *a transcript, certificate or any other credential* which is creditable towards a full higher education degree. Such a degree requires for completion a minimum of 3 years full-time attendance, or its part-time equivalent (e.g. bachelor programmes in the Anglo-saxon countries, academic or professional degrees in Europe, (e.g. licence in France) Diploma or State Exam in German speaking countries).

This definition excludes post-graduate training and non-degree courses, but includes non-traditional courses, such as part-time, evening, off-campus, and distance study programmes provided they meet the criteria listed above.

13    With respect to *continuing education* activities offered by higher education institutions (to be reported according to Part two, chapter B) courses should satisfy the two following criteria

a    they must require *application and registration*;

b    they must be of a *substantial nature*.

The latter criterion is introduced in order to exclude those activities which are very short in duration, (e.g. a one time lecture of one or two hours), thus not requiring a substantial commitment in terms of students' time.

14    It is hence suggested that in reporting the following *definitions of adult students in higher education are applied*:

a    *under Part two, Chapter A (full degree studies)* all students *aged 25 years and above*, who enrol in a *university or equivalent higher education institution* in order to *begin* a course the successful completion of which is creditable towards a full higher education degree;

b    *Under Part two, Chapter B (continuing education activities)* all students, *aged 25 years and above*, who enrol in a *course or programme of a substantial nature provided by a university or equivalent higher education institution*.

15    Although these definitions seem rather wide they might not adequately reflect the structures and classifications in all of the Member countries participating in the survey. Thus, countries wishing to deviate from one or other of the criterion of this definition in order to be able to

appropriately describe their situation are, of course, free to do so. In this case, however, it is requested that reasons are given why reporting under the above definitions was deemed unfeasible or inappropriate.

## IV Nature of Information Sought

16 While it can be assumed that the great bulk of the data and information requested does exist in some form or other, including publications, some of it may not be readily available. As the study addresses itself both to public and institutional policies and practice, replies will have to come from a variety of different sources. Furthermore, available data might have to be disaggregated or processed to fit the questions and classifications as applied here. However, consultations with experts from different countries suggest *that there are numerous sources and key contacts from whom relevant data can be obtained,* without necessitating the gathering of new data – which in any case could not be undertaken in view of the resources and time available for the completion of this project.

17 In some countries with a federal structure, policies for higher education are entirely, or primarily, the responsibility of the states or provinces (the US, Canada) and hence the response to adult demand for higher education varies considerably from one state or province to another. In these countries, aggregate surveys at the national level could mask significant differences between states (provinces) and it might therefore be more meaningful that surveys be either conducted at state (province) level alone, or that national surveys be complemented by surveys of a few states (provinces) which are regarded as either representative or which significantly differ from the others.

# Part Two: Country Data and Information

18 In the following, data and information are sought with respect to adult enrolment in higher education and to financial and organizational policies and practice regarding adult students. To enable the Secretariat to adequately interpret this information, som contextual information is also requested, especially regarding the higher education system as a whole as well as the non-academic adult education sector.

**19** In order to avoid that the survey be overfraught by lengthy and time consuming descriptions of the overall system, Member countries are invited to *make reference to existing material*, provided that it is attached, published or otherwise accessible.

**20** The survey is divided into two chapters. Chapter A concerns adult students enrolled in *full (first) degree programmes* while the focus in *Chapter B* is on adults seeking *continuing education* in higher education institutions.

**21** It must be re-emphasized that *the following grid of questions is not applicable in detail in any one country and should therefore be regarded as a checking list rather than a tight framework. Replies should therefore disregard those items which do not apply, and include others which are pertinent but not mentioned here.*